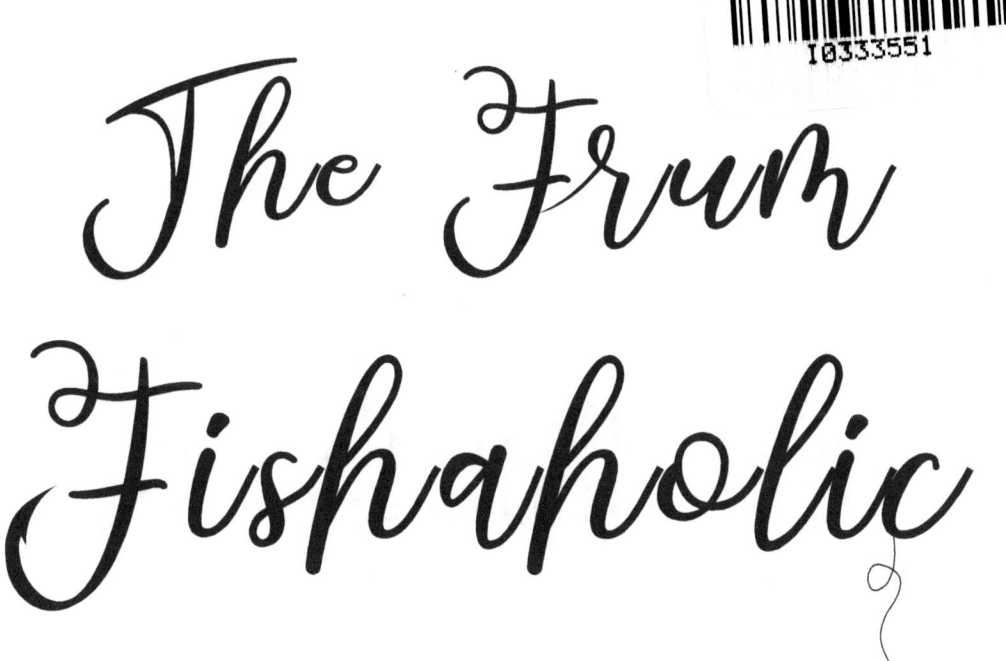

by

PHIL LUMBROSO

Copyright © 2024

All rights reserved.

All images are copyrighted and not to be used without permission.

All rights reserved. Without limiting the rights under copyrights reserved above, no part of this publication may be scanned, uploaded, reproduced, distributed, or transmitted in any form or by any means whatsoever without express prior written permission from both the author and publisher of this book—except in the case of brief quotations embodied in critical articles and reviews.

Thank you for supporting the author's rights.

Publisher: ThunderNet Inc

Electronic Version ISBN: 978-1-0689872-1-2

Printed Version ISBN: 978-1-0689872-0-5

בס'ד

Preface v

CHAPTER 1: The beginning 1

CHAPTER 2: Getting serious 11

CHAPTER 3: The carp craze 27

CHAPTER 4: Ice fishing 51

CHAPTER 5: Outfitters 71

CHAPTER 6: Online presence 91

CHAPTER 7: Travel 97

CHAPTER 8: Meaningful catches. 117

Epilogue 127

Preface

How does being frum (observant Jew) affect one's fishing? Simply put, in many more ways than one may think. I'm no rabbi, so anything I state in this book is purely my opinion, and for those of you that have more specific questions on how to reconcile fishing with halacha (Jewish code of law), my suggestion would be to check with your rabbi or rav.

For the most part, sport fishing isn't much of a frum Jew's sort of pastime. Save for a handful of friends and a few acquaintances that I've had the pleasure of fishing with, most of the outside world is clueless about the nuances of balancing a frum lifestyle with sport fishing. Which was why I decided to write this book, based on my personal experiences as a frum "fishaholic".

Before delving into my first attempt at authoring a book on my lifelong fishing addiction and experiences, a few thanks are in order.

First, I thank Hashem (God), creator of the world, for creating our amazing planet, its waterways, the fish we chase, as well as for giving me the knowledge, physical, and financial ability to have spent as much time fishing as I have. There is nothing besides Him.

לַה' הָאָרֶץ וּמְלוֹאָהּ תֵּבֵל וְיֹשְׁבֵי בָהּ
כִּי הוּא עַל יַמִּים יְסָדָהּ וְעַל נְהָרוֹת יְכוֹנְנֶהָ

The earth and everything in it are the Lord's; the world and those who dwell therein. For He founded it upon seas and established it upon rivers.

Next, I thank my dear father of blessed memory, who was the one who first put me on to sport fishing as a young child. Being a bit older than most fathers, and more nervous than some others, he had all the time and patience for me when it came to fishing. I just wish we could have fished together more often. Included, I thank my dear mother going along with my dad's plans, allowing us to go with him at young ages, as well as agreeing to us taking him out on weeklong trips in his later years. Next, I thank my brother, friends, and other fishing buddies, with whom I've had the pleasure of sharing the bank, boats, ice, and all the other crazy endeavors we've been through over the years. Some of you are mentioned by name, others just alluded to. Next, I'd like to thank my kids for coming along with me on so many outings from the time you were toddlers. I really hope that all the time we spent together will be remembered and appreciated throughout your lives.

Last but not least, I thank the love of my life, my amazing wife, for putting up with my fishing addiction over all these years. Behind every good fisherman, there is a very tolerant wife, often holding down the fort, while we pursue our dreams. I have seen too many instances where spouses got in the way of their man's fishing. No matter the reason, for the better or for worse, I'm not here to judge. But my wife has always been above it all, just happy to see me happy, no matter whether I got skunked, or had my best day on the water. Thanks again!

CHAPTER 1

The beginning

My first memories of fishing with my father were back when I was a young child. He had a few old rods in our basement locker, a tacklebox with a very basic mix of lures and terminal tackle, a landing net, and an old style metal double minnow bucket with chain. For most of his life, he primarily fished "old school" style, using live bait. Mainly earthworms he'd catch the night before the outing, or a mix of minnows, frogs or crayfish that were usually available at the local bait shops near our fishing spots.

I remember the excitement on the nights before our outings. We'd go down to get the gear ready, and then wait until after dark to go catch worms for bait in our back yard, using flashlights covered with red or orange cellophane, to avoid spooking them.

Though I was not a morning person at all, when it came to fishing or early Saturday morning cartoons, I was up before sunrise, waking my dad before his alarm clock would ring. We are Jewish, but we were non observant back in those days, so Saturdays were when most of our early fishing outings occurred. Much of our fishing was done at the Long Sault Parkway in Southeastern Ontario, about an hour's drive from where we lived in Montreal. We'd head out bright and early, often before sunrise, stopping for doughnuts at Tim Horton's, back before they were the huge chain they are today. My dad always swore by those, unequivocally calling them the best doughnuts we could buy.

I first remember catching some perch on the baited lines, but they were far and few in between. Hooking rocks on bottom, and massive bird's nest tangles that mono line created in the hands of an inexperienced kid like myself, were the norm. He must have spent a lot of time untangling and retying, and not being the most patient of people, he'd often get a bit nervous. Not in a bad way, but enough to where I eventually tried to avoid mentioning tangles or bird's nest until they were a hopeless mess.

Eventually, he introduced me to fishing lures, tying on a small red and white wooden Jitterbug. In addition to practice my casting, I was no longer worried about hooking bottom, nor getting fouled up in weeds, as it was a topwater lure fished on the surface. I still remember my first topwater fish, as if it were yesterday. I was casting shallow along a steep rock bank at the Mille Roches section of the Long Sault parkway. As usual, I watched my lure to try to make sure my retrieve was giving the crawling / gurgling action my dad suggested I maintain while retrieving the lure. In the gin clear water, I could see a smallmouth bass rise and chase my lure before exploding and crushing it at the surface. Not a big bass, it probably measured in the 10 to 12 inch range. But like-ly one of the most memorable bass I've caught over the many decades since then.

THE BEGINNING

My father and I, on Schroon Lake, NY around 1979-1980.

Eventually, my parents found their way to Jewish orthodoxy, a much more stringent version of religious practice then I had been accustomed to up until that point. I was put into a Jewish school, where we attended 6 classes days a week. Saturday was our day off school, but as orthodox Jews, it is forbidden for us to fish on the Shabbat. Instead, we spent it at the synagogue. Basically, we didn't have many opportunities to fish during the 10 months of the school year, except for a few days off school during spring and fall holidays. Summers were better, if we weren't away at sleep away camp. We got to fish with my dad on Sundays, as he had a tight weekday work schedule. My younger brother was born five years after me, so he eventually joined us on our outings as well. In between, we had to content ourselves by watching some fishing shows on TV such as Bob Izumi's Real fishing show, the original Canadian Sportfishing show with Italo and Henry, and Jean Pagé on RDS in French.

As I got a bit older, around the age of fifteen, I got to start fishing on my own. We were sent away to Gan Israel, a Jewish orthodox sleep away summer camp in the upper Laurentians, which was located on a decent sized lake. Back in those days, the lake was sparsely populated, and the fish population was still quite dense. While younger kids were strictly prohibited from getting anywhere near the water outside of supervised activities, teenagers had more leeway. I spent a few summers shore fishing the lake with a variety of lures, mainly topwaters, which are still my favorite to date. Hundreds of rock bass, mixed in with the occasional largemouth or smallmouth bass, and some sunfish. On rare occasions, perch or trout, when I'd switch up to using whatever bait I could forage, or casting small spinners. I easily fished 5-6 days per week, though only for a few hours per day, but enough to gain a lot of valuable casting experience.

My mom and siblings with me on visiting day at summer camp, around 1987 or 1988.

THE BEGINNING

As my dad got older and busier with a business he had started later in life, the frequency of our fishing outings slowed down considerably. In my late teens, I just about stopped fishing for a few years, opting instead to hang around or party with friends, and eventually, with the love of my life that I ended up marrying.

Life moved forward. I got married relatively early, just before my 21st birthday. My eldest son Ari was born just over one year later, followed by my first daughter Chani, a couple years later. At the time, I again found myself in a situation that didn't lend itself to much fishing time, working long shifts during a 6 day work week, with only Saturday's off. As an observant Orthodox Jew, fishing or working on Saturdays is strictly forbidden and out of the question.

Due to my long work shifts, I started feeling bad about the fact that I didn't have much time to spend with my young children. Sundays were my only chance of getting off a few hours earlier than normal, and on one particular Sunday around 1997, I took my son Ari out for his first outing. A cheap $10 rod and reel set, with a few dug up worms on the way out, we hit a spot about 20 minutes drive from my home in Montreal. Barely 2 years old at the time, it didn't take him long to get hooked on fishing, and the outdoors in general.

My eldest son Ari and I on one of hist first outings.

That outing turned out to be a new renewal for myself, as my son was just itching to get out to fish with me again. It was a win-win situation, as my wife was home with two younger children every day, she was happy for me to take him, and eventually my daughter as well out with me, so she could get much needed breaks to relax and have some time for herself.

Strange as it may sound, she never wanted to come along with us on our outings. This went on for a while, so I stopped bothering to invite her. One day, 16 years after we were married, seemingly out of the blue, she asks "how come you never take me fishing"? I obliged, and started taking her along for some shore fishing, occasionally for bass, but usually for carp, which don't require her to do much except from grabbing the line that goes off, and fighting the fish. We've had quite a few fishing dates since then.

My wife and I on one of our dates, this big carp was her first 30+ lbs.

As I started going out with my kids whenever I could find the time, inviting my dad, brother, nephew, and cousins to join whenever they could as well, so we'd get some really nice family time together, doing what we enjoyed most.

In time, my family kept growing, and my schedule freed itself up, due to a new career and business that I started. With a more flexible schedule, I was now able to get out to fish with my younger kids more often. We welcomed three more sons between 2000 and 2005, Avi, Levi and Eli. Starting each one off fishing around the age of 2 years old, friends my age would laugh when I was changing diapers during outings. Another daughter and son (Chaya and Zev), joined a few years later.

My kids enjoyed lots of time on the water in their younger years.

There is something to be said about initroducing young children to the outdoors, and fishing in particular. Growing up in a Jewish Hasidic area, it is quite rare for kids to experience it, especially nowadays, where modern technology such as video games, tablets, etc. often get in the way. That simple innocence and fascination interacting with other living creatures not found in a big city, or simply watching a few fresh caught fish swimming around in a bucket. The excitement of watching a bobber sink below the surface, or a fish exploding on the surface to crush a topwater lure. Etc, etc.

Kids being kids outdoors, it's not always about only catching fish.

While many of my day trips involved taking my young kids fishing with me, I had also started broadening my fishing horizons, and planning some short overnight fishing trips. Being very tight with money in those days, I opted for the cheapest possible solution, namely, finding campgrounds that rented boats, pitching a tent with a couple friends for a few nights, and fishing from dawn to dusk.

Those trips weren't the most successful, for a variety of reasons. The lack of knowledge, rudimentary equipment like canoes or rowboats without any electronics (not that we'd have known how to use them), and general lack of trophy fish in the small rivers or lake adjacent to the campgrounds we stayed at. The old clunker 9 hp motor that was much older than us, had its various moods when it came to starting up. Still, those trips were very memorable, and the excitement of trying new spots each time around was enough to keep us going in between trips.

Most of these early camping trips were attended by myself, my brother David, and my good friend Raphy. Our varying schedules made it tricky to align the three of us being able to attend all trips together, but somehow we made it work every now and then. Always good times, and great memories. Eventually some legendary fishing tales, though not necessarily about the fish.

My friend Raphy and I during one of our early camping trips in 1997. Cost around $10 per night.

Eventually, my brother got a cheap sonar unit, and we had a bit more insight as to what we were doing. A few trips back to the lake where I had gone to sleep away camp were nice. One of the lake locals was nice enough to rent his rowboat to us, we'd get up there bright and early, mount the old motor and sonar, and spend the day reminiscing and fishing the waters where we once only speculated on what lay below.

One such occasion still makes me laugh every time I tell it, even though it's been over a couple decades since it happened. As previously mentioned, back when the three of us we still working long hours in various jobs, schedules were tough to align, trips often being planned many weeks in advance in order to ensure we could all attend.

David, Raphy, and myself, all agreed to go out on a long day trip, on a given Sunday, must have been in July or August. The plan was to try fishing the Du Lievre River for the first time, renting a boat from a local spot that opened at 7:00 AM. As it was at least a 2.5 hour drive to get there, we planned to leave well before sunrise, fish until dark, and get back home after 10 PM.

A week or two before the outing, my cousin decided to make his henna/engagement party on the day of our outing. As annoying as it sounded, we were going to have cut the trip short, leaving around 4:00 pm in order to make it back to Montreal for the 7:00 PM event.

On the day of the outing, we made sure to be out the door extra early. My brother packed his old Johnson outboard motor in his car, and we were there well in time as planned. Fishing was going well enough. We landed a mix of bass, pike, and some jumbo perch. As the afternoon rolled in, we decided to make our way downstream. Somewhere around 3 pm, with about 1 hour left in the planned outing, we came across a decent sized bridge.

THE BEGINNING

Figuring it would provide nice shade for ourselves and the fish on a hot sunny day, we anchored under the bridge. Sure enough, on the first cast, I landed a walleye, followed up by my brother landing one as well. Up until that point, neither of us had ever landed any walleyes. The bite continued, as Raphy (not much of a fisherman) started cautioning us that it was time to start heading back. My brother started with the infamous "one more cast" line, and being that we were in a boat with his motor, and drove up in his car, there wasn't much more to add. Next thing we know, we're unloading the boat around 7:30 PM, and still facing at least a 3 hour drive home in traffic. This was well before the times of being able to call anyone, as none of us, nor the guests at the party, had cel phones. Needless to say, we arrived well after the party ended, restaurant was closed as it was nearly midnight. I laid all the blame on my brother, and still do, every time my cousin and I laugh about it.

CHAPTER 2

Getting serious

For starters, let us delve into the question of whether or not one is permitted to sport fish according to strict Jewish law. The main reason to abstain from sport fishing would be to avoid causing unnecessary pain to a living creature. It is definitely permissible to catch fish for the table, and learning how to identify kosher species, is a positive mitzvah. While relatively simple for most species, there are the occasional oddities that are questionable, such as freshwater ling, and bowfins.

Walleye are one of the tastiest kosher freshwater species in Canada.

Catch and release fishing becomes more of a grey area. Though it is possible that many fish don't feel pain, most would agree that fighting a fish, landing and releasing it, can still cause undue stress or damage to it. On the flip side, there are likely loopholes one can use in order to justify fishing for sport.

In my case, I did part time work as a fishing guide for a number of years, which again, is permissible without any issues. Keeping on top of the fish, and ensuring your customers get what they paid for, inevitably will entail the need to practice quite often, keeping my skills sharp, and constantly learning more about the fish we chase. As well, I used my fishing habits to earn some extra income through my web site, blog, and eventually, to write this book.

Seemingly, much of the fishing I do should be well within the legal guidelines of Judaism. There are some cases that are likely more sketchy. Big game fishing comes to mind. Hooking a giant fish purely for the fun of a crazy battle, with no intention of harvesting it. I may be on the wrong side of halacha on these trips, but in my simple (and biased) mind, there are other parts to the equation.

I often hear the term "serious fisherman" being thrown around in conversation. Over the years, I've come to the realization, that as with many other things in life, there are levels to this game. In the eyes of a non angler with little to no experience, nor true knowledge of what fishing is about, an occasional fisherman may seem "serious", especially if they own a rod, and manage to catch some fish every now and then. On the flip side, to a fishing aficionado, the term "serious", has a far different meaning.

Then of course, there is an intersection where mindset hits reality. Some people aren't able to make or afford the time to fish as much as they may want to, even though their skill level and desire to do so, can be just as intense as one that may own a nice fishing boat and have time to fish a few times a week. Basically, there are many factors that line up to create a "serious" fisherman, at least in my humble opinion.

I can't really pinpoint where my transition occurred, or if one even occurred at all. It may just be an accumulation of experience, leading to better skills, which intersected with more free time, at the right times. Add the burning desire to get out to explore new waterways, species, and techniques, to the hope of landing the biggest one ever, with every cast. Makes for a recipe of myriads of hours spent doing what we enjoy most.

At some point in the early 2000's, I found myself self employed, after about 8-9 years of mainly working jobs with office hours. With a highly flexible schedule, I was now able to start putting in more time into my fishing obsession. The time I was putting in didn't take long to pay off. Within a couple years, I was out fishing new spots with both new and old fishing buddies on a regular basis, in addition to hiring guides every now and then, or going on 4-5 day fishing trips at outfitters.

As opposed to our old style camping trips staying in tents, we had upgraded to renting fishing cabins on better waterways, for longer periods of time, than during our less comfortable tent trips. The experience factor grew exponentially, as we fed off each others' experiences, and our catch rates, sizes, and variety of species followed along.

As with any other facet in life, occasionally, one simple / seemingly minute event, can lead to much more, later down the road. Case in point, my good friend Jimmy.

Jimmy and I first met as kids attending Shabbat services at our synagogue. We were the only kids there that fished, aside from our siblings. His dad is a lifelong outdoorsman, as well as a dedicated fly fisherman. We fished together as kids a few times, but eventually lost contact with each other for a good 15 years or so, when he moved to a different neighborhood.

On an early June evening around 2005 or 2006, I was invited to a charity golf tournament, benefitting my daughter's school (Beth Rivka). The tournament had been going on for a few years by then, but as I don't golf, I was never interested in attending. The director suggested that I come just for the cocktails and fundraising dinner after the tournament, so I figured I'd surprise my wife with the dinner date.

During the course of the meal, the director proceeded with the awards ceremony. With apparently no shock to any of the attendees, Jimmy and his team won the tournament hands down, as they were the reigning champions for a while. After accepting his award, I went to congratulate him, and proceeded to catch up on old times. I learned that he specialized in making custom made golf clubs, and spent much of his summers playing daily rounds of golf with his customers. With that amount of experience, it was little wonder that his team did so well, being that most of the rest of the playing field was made up of mostly Chassidic rabbis that barely knew how to swing a club.

More importantly, we got to talking about fishing. During the course of our conversation, he mentioned how much he missed fishing, and spent most of his time golfing, as that was what most of his friends and customers did. Luckily, I had just booked a deluxe cabin at Mijocama outfitter, as my brother and I had planned to bring my father up there for the first time, later that month. Knowing that I had a lot of extra room, I invited him to come up to join us with his eldest son. He didn't need much convincing, and after getting the OK from his wife, he joined us.

Without going into more details about the outfitter (which will come in a later chapter), Jimmy and I hit it off so well, that we started fishing together on a steady basis. Much to the chagrin of his golf game, he started putting in more time fishing with me instead.

Jimmy's experience and fishing skill set were/are far superior to mine. While I did a lot of stationary multi species shore fishing using live bait, he was mainly into casting lures. While both were efficient tactics, there were times and areas where using live bait wasn't an option. Eventually, I joined the bandwagon, and Jimmy and I decided to invest in a small motorboat together. We found a small boat for sale at Mac's Marina in South Lancaster, where one of the workers who was retiring was selling his boat. We bought the small 14 foot flat bottomed Cadormat, that came with a 25HP Mariner 2 stroke outboard. Plenty of power for a small boat that size, and it was very stable in calm water. We added a rudimentary sonar unit to help us with depths and trolling, along with a few other minor modifications.

The purchase of the boat came along with the commitment Jimmy and I had, namely, to put the boat to good use. We started fishing on our boat 1-2 times per week, for full days at a time. As the boat didn't come with a trailer, we just docked it at Mac's marina every season. This avoided the need for us to store, trailer, and launch the boat each time we wanted to fish. Instead, we had the ease of driving up to our dock, throwing some rods and cold beer onto the boat, and off we went.

Being on the St Lawrence River, we weren't always lucky enough to have weather calm enough to keep fishing there. Luckily for us, the Raisin River feeds into the St Lawrence very close to the marina, so as soon as the wind picked up, it was up the calm, muddier waters of the Raisin we headed to fish. Back then, the river still had some crazy runs of smallmouth bass, and big walleyes in the spring, as well as insane numbers of spawning bullheads. Resident largemouth bass, crappies, bluegills and pike were abundant, as were long nose gars sunning themselves near the surface, on hot, mid summer days.

For 4 seasons, Jimmy and I shared the boat, and during that time, must have easily fished over 100 days from that boat, in addition to many days spent shore fishing.

Around the same time, I had just started fishing for carp (more on that in the carp chapter). My primary spot was near Long Sault, about 25 minutes' drive from where our boat was docked in Lancaster. It didn't take long for Jimmy to get into carping as well, though to a lesser level than myself. As my spot had a low bridge we could get under incase of rain, we often mixed our day trips between the boat and shore fishing, typically when forecast called for rainy mornings and clearing evenings.

Jimmy also started coming along on our yearly trips to Mijocama for the bass opener, eventually bringing up a growing number of family and friends. Nearly 2 decades later, we now occupy most of the cabins in the camp during our week long stays at Mijocama.

My brother, Dad obm, Jimmy and Albert obm, Mijocama 2006.

While I have kept large numbers of fish for the table over the years, I've released far more than I've kept. Much of my open water fishing is done in the Montreal and surrounding area, where the waterways are more polluted some many of the pristine forest lakes I have had the privilege of fishing. Living smack in the middle of a large frum community where everyone knows everyone, it's no secret that I'm an avid angler. For the most part, most people don't ask me too many questions about fishing, but when they do, the most common response is shock when they hear that I don't keep most of what I catch.

Occasionally, my neighbors will ask me to bring them some fish. Early on, I didn't think much of it, until they (and I) realized that they would have to clean the fish. While this was once a common skill for the average shtetl housewife, today's women are more likely to freak out, than to know how to use a fillet knife.

My late father had a close friend who was the Rav (rabbi) of the shul (synagogue) he prayed at. Once in a while, we'd bring him some fish from one of our fishing trips, typically after I cleaned and deboned them. At some point, the Rav had asked me to bring him some fish from some of my shorter day trips around home. Sometimes carp, pike at other times. Seems like he really had a preference for pike, and being that his wife was retired, he probably figured she'd be fine cleaning them.

One spring day, Jimmy and I went out to troll for pike. We did quite well, starting off by landing pike on every pass we trolled. Figuring that I'd stock his freezer for the season, we kept a 6 pike bag limit in the livewell of Jimmy's new boat. As the Rav lived near my house, I figured I'd drop the fish off at his place on my way home. We pulled up at his house, I dumped the fish into a couple large garbage bags, and handed them to the happy old couple.

A couple days later, I ran into the Rav who had quite the story to tell. Apparently, I forgot to knock out the pike before bagging them for him. Guess I wasn't thinking much of it, but when they opened the bags, the slimy pikes started flapping, and he ended up with him and his wife chasing around the slimy fish jumping all over the kitchen floor with a hammer. He also didn't realize that his wife's filleting skills weren't up to par, and nor were the knives they had…

Though Jimmy's impact on my fishing skill level was significant, it was by far not the only one. My younger brother David and I fished many day trips, as well as dawn to dusk trips to campgrounds, and eventually outfitters as well. Probably many dozens of days, if not in the hundreds were shared between us. Along with all the good times, came along sibling rivalry and mandatory trash talk.

Unfortunately for us, his fishing obsession waned when he took over my dad's business, and simply got too busy to be able to put in any serious time fishing, due to the more important duties of running his business, which demanded his constant presence there. He still does join us during some of our yearly trips to Mijocama or the occasional day trip, and his boys both enjoy fishing as well. Guess it's in the blood...

Another important figure in my fishing journey, is my friend Mike. We first met when Jimmy and I hired him to take us out for our first guided musky outing, mainly to get an idea of how it's done. As I had recently launched my website (more on that in the FreshwaterPhil chapter), I posted pics of our outing, and eventually started putting Mike in touch with new customers. Every now and then, Mike invited me out to fish with him, sometimes for multispecies, other times on ice, where I learned a lot about ice fishing from him.

Over the years, Mike and I have become good friends, we've fished together dozens of times, from bass, pike and walleye outings with some crazy numbers, to giant muskies in the St Lawrence River, to some crazy lake trout action on Lake Champlain in New York, after ice out.

Any time I get the itch for some crazy big game adventure, Mike steps up to the plate. Over the years, we've fished for big hammerhead sharks in Florida's Gulf Stream, the Gulf of Mexico for Goliath grouper, and the world famous Fraser River in British Columbia for giant white sturgeon.

Mike and I on our first saltwater trip together, Cape Coral FL, 2016.

Many other professional guides and top notch anglers I've shared the water with, have provided many new learning experiences as well. There a simply too many to mention by name. Even newbies with lower skill levels and much less experience than myself, will often provide some new insights, which I often come to realize on my own, without them even thinking much of it.

Case in point, my kids. As I have 7 children, most of whom have been actively fishing since they were in diapers, I have fished hundreds of days with my kids, often a few of them at a time. Teaching them how to accurately cast lures near sunken logs along the shore, or showing them how to effectively fight big carp on 12 foot rods, over and over again, trip after trip. All that fishing sort of just rubs off and soaks in, to where certain things become almost second nature to me when it comes to fishing.

Some nice catches on guided fishing trips over the years.

I often like to try to break down various stages of one's likely fishing experience, while at the same time, trying to quantify different levels of what I would consider being a "serious" fisherman.

I'll usually start with the simplistic approach of how many days a person devotes to fishing, even if for only a few hours at a time. When it comes to myself, I have had a good number of seasons that I've managed to fish on over 100 days per calendar year (ice fishing is included). While I realize that many serious anglers don't have that amount of time to put in, when I do run into people that put more time into fishing than I do, my respect for those individuals as seasoned anglers is a no brainer.

Next, I move onto the style or lifestyle of fishing that our candidate for "serious" fisherman can have. For example, does one need to own a boat in order to qualify as serious? Well, I don't anymore, having sold my boat in 2009. Still, I fish a lot more now, so I don't think I'm disqualified. Perhaps one has crazy fly fishing skills, another may have less time but more money to spend on crazy fishing adventures across the globe, to where they can spend more money on a couple fishing trips, than I can spend in a full decade of fishing. I'd say they all qualify as well.

Lastly, I think of individual mindset. Most of us start of fishing as kids, where the main focus is (and should be) numbers. Kids in the 2-5 year old age bracket have shorter attention spans, and need constant action to avoid getting bored. Catching large numbers of panfish like perch, sunfish, and rock bass, will both keep them occupied, and get them started acquiring fishing skills. Next stage, is starting to go after game fish, like bass, pike, walleye, etc. These are bigger fish, that are generally harder to come by, but increase in size and ensuing battles usually counters the drop in numbers.

Some anglers stop there, and will be happy to spend their day fishing for good numbers of mid sized fish, while others will move along to the next level of trying to target bigger trophy fish. While many "serious" anglers will opt to spend the time needed to get the results being sought, it's safe to say that it's extremely rare to find anyone less than serious join this category, at least not on a regular basis.

Lastly, there are the real professionals. These are the fishing guides, tournament anglers, fishing TV show celebrities, etc. People that fish in order to earn a living in the sport fishing industry.

Of course, this discussion is greatly hypothetical, and also simply based on my personal views. In the big scheme of things, it doesn't really matter, nor affect much at all. Any given moment out on the water, from the serenity, to the sights of sunrises and sunsets, to the smell of the woods, to the chirping birds and calling loons, all add up to moments that shape our personal experience with the great outdoors where our favorite pastime is practiced.

At some point, I realized that fishing isn't just about the results, it's also about the "how". For example, I may choose to forgo an almost certain good day of a particular type of fishing, in order to try to achieve another quest. Namely, trying new spots, species, and techniques.

My rule of thumb is, that if I'm not making a new spot, I'm eliminating one. Same goes for techniques. I know that I wouldn't be catching fish sitting on my couch, therefore I choose to hit a new lake. If I now come across any good fishing there, I've made myself a spot that can potentially pay off for many years to come. At worst, if the catch levels are horrendous, I can safely say that the spot won't be high on my go to list, especially if I return again, and don't do any better the second time around.

Occasionally, some of these outings can pay off in ways other than expected. I've found some amazing summer carp fishing spots by first fishing them on ice for other species, and I've found some very good ice fishing spots fishing both from the shore, or from my float tube.

Same goes for multispecies, especially with the variety of fish we have around Montreal. Though I might have evolved into a much better bass fisherman had I devoted all my fishing time to chasing bass, I feel like I'd be missing out on the variety and styles needed to catch other species like carp, sturgeon, etc.

I found a great carp spot while ice fishing, and a great ice fishing spot while float tubing.

Back in 2008, I started keeping a log of all my fishing outings. Recording important factors such as location, date, species/sizes caught, lures used, solunar tables, times of day, outer and water temps, sun/cloud cover, wind speed/direction, and general comments, have all provided great reference for me to be able to pattern bites for the various species I target. Additionally, I have accurate information on the number of outings I do, and number of fish / species I catch every season.

In a nutshell, a serious fisherman will somehow find/make the necessary time to get out and fish, more often than not. Then, there is the next level of addiction to the sport, namely, one that fishes whenever possible, opting to fish over all other possible pastimes, excursions, trips, or vacations.

Speaking for myself, I can safely say that the vast majority of vacations I've been on in the past couple decades have involved fishing, often at the detriment of what others perceived as more "worthy" or important pursuits given the circumstances.

A few examples that my family can attest to:

Back in 2013, my in laws bought a lake front house in the Rocky Mountains in Colorado. Most of the rest of the family enjoys skiing, so they typically visited during the winter. I made my first trip out there during the summer, along with my wife, 3 of our kids, and my brother in law with his family. Being the adventurous types, they mapped out various hikes, jeep trails, and other tourist destinations to visit every day. I just sat watching the lake from the hilltop view, keeping a rod on hand. Every now and then, I when I noticed a hatch followed by feeding activity, I'd step out to fish for 30 to 60 minutes or so, then come back inside. Day after day, they planned activities, while I opted to watch the kids and take them out to fish with me. Eventually, my brother in law flat out asked me whether or not I was interesting in doing anything else besides fishing, to which my answer was "obviously not".

A view Trout Lake Colorado from my in law's house.

A few years later, my wife and I went to the Island of Kauai, in Hawaii. My sister in law planned her wedding there, and our immediate family all gathered in the resort town of Poipu Beach for the weeklong trip. While they filled most of their days exploring the island's jungles, hiking trails, and peaks, I brought along some fishing gear, and spent most of my free time during the days, casting into the ocean, and still fishing the beach during the night. I needed a fair bit of convincing to do anything else during the entire trip, I think a helicopter tour of the island, was the only family based activity I participated in during the entire trip.

Shore fished day and night during my 2018 trip to Kauai.

The situation repeated itself again on a 2023 trip to Bermuda. Again, my in laws planned a family cruise to the Island. I brought along a travel rod, and after sailing for 3 days from New York City, I was ready to start fishing as soon as we docked. The 30+ other people in our group spent 3 days touring Bermuda by moped, ferry, and taxi, visiting beaches, lagoons, and all of the Island's other tourist destinations, while I never even made it out of the harbor. 3 days of shore fishing on foot, in the vicinity of where the cruise ship was docked, I barely made it to more than a mile or so, as the fishing was too tempting to leave.

DIY shore fishing in Bermuda in 2023 was very productive.

The only vacation that I chose not to fish on, was a trip to Israel back in 2003. It was a religious trip, a pilgrimage of sorts. Knowing that I was making my way halfway across the planet to visit and tour most of the tiny country, fishing would have kept me from doing most of the prayers, and visiting holy sites/shrines while I was there. Outside of that trip, any travel to new destinations, whether for business or pleasure, will most likely contain some sort of fishing, as long as it's feasible.

CHAPTER 3

The carp craze

It has been said that one man's trash is another's treasure. That has held true in regards to carp fishing in Canada, more so than any other species.

Growing up, we all knew that some giant carp existed in many of the waterways we fished, but in particular, the St Lawrence River. We'd often find some bloated dead carp floating near the shores, or sometimes out in open water. I often wondered what it would be like to catch one of those big carp. Over and over again, I was told by just about everyone I mentioned them to, that they were "trash fish". Deemed useless, invasive, and thought to devour the eggs of other sport fish, they remained untargeted by sport fishermen, save for maybe a few bow fishermen that would kill spawning giants when they were at their most vulnerable stage, only to use them as fertilizer at best, or simply leave them to rot on shores or garbage dumps. Back then, little did any of us here in North America know that they were considered a huge sport fish overseas, even bigger than the bass fishing industry was here.

I first remember seeing carp swimming in the gin clear waters around the Long Sault parkway. For reasons unknown to me at the time, I could never get them to hit or even chase any lures I threw at them. They simply just swam away slowly, or sometimes darted if they were spooked. I didn't give them much thought, up until my early thirties.

At that time, I was a attending an old synagogue for morning services. I was by far the youngest of the dozen or so of us that showed up every morning, most others were between the ages of sixty, going into their mid nineties. Albert was a senior citizen whom I fished with at summer camp, during in my teens. He had been working in their kitchen at that time, but now we were 15 years later, and he was working part time at a hospital nearby.

Every now and then, after morning services, we'd talk a bit about fishing. One morning, another elderly member named Aaron, chimed into to our conversation. He was a lifelong fisherman, now in his early retirement years. The three of us hit it off well, and one day Aaron started talking about all the carp he used to catch. My first reaction was to call them a trash fish, to which he replied, "just wait until you catch one".

That was enough to get me slightly intrigued. We set up a fishing date for the three of us to try his carp spot. I was still pretty skeptical, so I brought long a small tacklebox, as well as a minnow bucket. The zone we fished at in Southeast Ontario still allowed for the use of perch as live bait back then, and knowing that there was a decent pike population at the spot, I figured I'd just bait fresh caught perch under a bobber for pike, while Aaron fished for carp.

Aaron's setup was barebones, old school. Some canned corn threaded onto a baitholder hook, fished on bottom with the help of a small sinker. I can't remember whether or not he also threw in some corn by hand, but I did my own thing, chasing perch for bait. I eventually caught a few perch for my minnow bucket, and managed to land some decent pike on the perch baited line. Aaron on the other hand, got skunked, Not even a nibble all day, despite us seeing a lot of carp surfacing and jumping, throughout the day. I figured he must have been exaggerating his fishing tales, and didn't think much of carp again.

Having confirmed that there was a decent pike and smaller walleye population at the spot, as well as easy access and a low bridge to get under in case of rain or excessive sun, I started going there ever once in a while with my kids. Plenty of panfish to keep them busy, while we waited for pike to hit our lines baited with live perch under bobbers.

One funny pike story at that spot sticks out a bit more than others. It must have been early to mid May, just after pike season opened in that zone. I was with my older son Ari, who was still a young child at the time. Water temp was still quite cold, and we were wearing heavy sweaters despite the sunny conditions. One of the bobbers started moving against the slight current, so we knew a pike had taken the live perch we baited. Unfortunately, it was quite close to the concrete bridge piling, and when I set the hook, the braided line snapped from abrasion on the piling. A good 10 to 15 minutes later, I saw the bobber swimming around not far from where I originally hooked the fish. I tried casting a lure to snag the bobber, but was unsuccessful. After a few minutes, I proceeded to strip down to my underwear, hop into the frigid water, swim out to grab the bobber, and swam back to shore with the pike still hooked.

Pike fishing at the spot went on until 2006, when I returned to fish there with my friend Jimmy. By then, the pike had started becoming more scarce, and he and I ended up getting skunked that day. However, the hundreds of jumping carp peaked my interest again, and I resolved to go back the following day, as my wife and kids were away visiting my in laws in the USA.

Jimmy couldn't make it the following day, so I headed out solo. In contrast to the hot sunny weather we enjoyed the previous day, I was now driving through intermittent, violent thunderstorms. That didn't have me too worried, as I knew I'd have cover under the bridge, and being in my bathing suit and water shoes, I didn't care much if I did get soaked, as we were still in a mid August heat wave.

I baited my line with corn, much the way I saw Aaron do to a few years before. I cast pretty close to shore, and threw in a handful or two of canned corn in the vicinity of my baited hook. I set my rod down in some rocks nearby, and sat down to wait. Within 10-15 minutes, my rod suddenly took off into the river! Luckily, I was close enough to jump in after it and grab it, but my line got cut in the rocks after a few of the strongest, blistering runs I had ever experienced!

I re-tied my line, cast out to the same spot, and sure enough, within minutes, I had another carp on the line. Same result, line cut in the rocks. Rinse, repeat, I lost two more back to back carp right after that, so I was now 0 out of 4 carp landed, and getting a bit frustrated. Someone fishing nearby saw what happened, and mentioned that carp need to be fished using a much looser drag setting, to lessen the chances of broken or cut lines. I obliged, and sure enough, I proceeded to land the next 5 carp I hooked. It didn't take any more than that, I was totally hooked!

The carp weren't big by any standards, most ranged in the 9 to 11 lbs class. However, when I had been used to catching bass or pike that are generally much smaller, these carp were a huge upgrade. Knowing that there were some giants pushing 40+ lbs in the St Lawrence, I could only begin to imagine the endless possibilities. Best of all, carp fishing didn't require a boat, nor any fancy or expensive gear, and canned corn was just about the simplest / cheapest bait one could use.

Growing up, my late grandfather use to love eating carp, as they were considered a delicacy back in Hungary, were he was originally from. Knowing that many people in my community were from Eastern European origin, I decided to keep those few carp, and offer it to a relatively poor rabbi with a large family to feed. While he was quite happy with all the meat, I didn't consider the fact that he, nor his wife, were too interested in cleaning carp. Luckily for them, the local fish monger was nice enough to do it for them.

My first few carp in 2006, back when I knew nothing about carp fishing. I had considered them a "trash fish" up until that point.

After arriving back home and getting cleaned up, I called Jimmy all excited about my newfound success. I invited him out for my next outing, and brought along a couple of my kids as well. Being that Ontario only allowed one rod per person for carping in those days, more kids meant more rods, which gave us a better shot at landing more fish. Sure enough, we all caught some carp, with the biggest going about 15 lbs. Though Jimmy really doesn't enjoy still fishing too much, the excuse of waiting for a few big fish to bite while downing some cold beers, suited us just fine.

To me, carp were no longer the trash fish I had originally thought them to be. They were big, strong, abundant, and relatively untargeted by just about anyone that I had fished with up until that point. Aaron was happy to learn that I had finally got into some carp at his spot, and we eventually got out to fish for them together.

Eventually, we refined our methods a bit, using heavier line, bigger reels (eventually baitrunners), rods holder and bells to hear the rods going off if we were further away from them.

Soon enough, I started noticing other carpers fishing in the same area. Most of them using strange looking gear, and mainly speaking in thick British accents. I eventually learned, that the Long Sault area was one of Canada's carp fishing epicenters. Just down the road from my spot, an Englishman named Jeff Vaughan, had purchased the Long Sault Motel, and set up a carp guiding operation there.

Apparently, he had owned some carp specific tackle shops in the United Kingdom, where carpers often paid thousands of pounds to fish in pre-stocked carp ponds, after being on waiting lists for possibly years. Jeff had visited Long Sault at some point, and was so impressed by the sheer quantity of untouched wild carp, that he knew he had stumbled onto a gold mine. Quite literally, as carp are golden in color, and the largest members of the goldfish family…

Jeff bought the motel, and set up the Canadian Carp club as his operation. His British customers were shocked to hear tales of the amazing carp fishing holidays to be had in Canada, at a fraction of the price they would pay back home, and where they could easily catch more fish in a few hours of a good bite, than in a week of fishing on some over pressured, stocked pond back home.

Jeff's wife ran the kitchen and room service, while Jeff ran the fishing operations and tackle rental shop based in the motel. As part of his operation, they used a barge filled with hundreds of lbs of presoaked corn, to pre-bait spots where they would then set the customers up on, to fish 10 to 12 hour shifts.

To us, these Brits and their Euro style carp fishing systems seemed over the top, and kind of odd.

Setting extra long rods into rods pods with bite alarms, oversized landing nets, and their extreme carp care methods, were all previously unheard of by any of us locals. Especially myself, who harvested many of my early caught carp for a fellow that ran an organization that feeds poor people in my area. He was nice enough to clean them in his garage for a while, but it didn't take long for him to get fed up and he asked me to stop bringing carp after I haphazardly dropped off a bin with a good dozen or so carp at his door one evening.

Within a couple seasons, I had started doing some part time guiding for carp. My first customers were from Austria. One of them was a professional carper back home, and brought along his Euro style gear. They hired me just to show them some spots, more than for my perceived "expertise". He actually mentioned that my gear and tactics were so primitive, that they were laughable by their standards. Sure enough, he hooked into 3 carp within the first 15 minutes or so of our outing, using boilies baited on hair rigs.

Seeing his success, I learned how to tie my own hair rigs, and bought some boilies from Carpins, a local carp supply shop nearby. Almost immediately, my catch rates increased, as did the average size of the carp I was catching. Fast forward a couple more seasons, and I started making my own boilies. As I had young kids at home eager to earn a few bucks, I took advantage of the cheap labor. Furthermore, they were excited to fish with the home made boilies, which allowed me to test various formulas and flavors more efficiently, due to the multiple rods I was able to fish with every time they came along.

Eventually, I stopped buying boilies, and fished exclusively using my home made versions. Besides for being more rewarding, I was able to sell some locally, which just about paid for all of the ones for personal use. They caught more fish, and also gave me personal satisfaction every time my kids or paying customers caught carp on the boilies I had formulated.

While I've had my share of interesting customers over the dozen or so years while I was guiding for carp, a couple come to mind. The first one was a fellow from the United Kingdom that called me to book a trip aging father, who was coming to visit from there. Early on the day of the outing, we met up at sunrise to get their fishing licenses. He had mentioned his father having trouble walking and breathing, and he was hooked up to an oxygen tank to help him breathe.

Knowing that access to my spot required climbing down some steep rocks, I advised against doing so, especially as it was raining, and the rocks were slipperier than normal. I suggested an alternate spot, where we would be able to drive right up to the waterfront, and fish from the comfort of a dry car. Having to drive by my first spot on the way there, I figured I'd stop and show it to them anyway. When we arrived at my spot, I pulled over to park. We stepped out of the car, to witness the largest carp spawn I have ever seen.

When carp spawn, they do so based on the water's temperature sometime in the late spring. A few small males typically circle a bigger female at the surface of the water. During most years, the spawn is sporadically spread out over a good 7-10 day period. On rare occasions, they all spawn within a day or two, which is what must have occurred that morning.

The elder father's eyes nearly popped out of his head, as he had never seen thousands of wild carp anywhere. He insisted that we stay at the spot, despite my mentioning to him that spawning carp are less likely to feed, and that there was a treacherous climb down to the waterfront.

His son came down to assess the situation, and to my surprise, mentioned that he would carry his aging dad down the rocks. He did so, while I set up the rods. Next issue was the rain, which was only getting heavier. I set up the chairs under the bridge out of the rain, but that meant that we would need to run out on the wet rocks, to grab any lines going off. As this trip was all about his dad, he wanted his dad to be the one to get the rods first. As a solution, he put his dad in a chair right by the rods in the rain, and proceeded to hold an umbrella over him until the fish would bite.

Not surprisingly, the bite was slow as could be. When carp are spawning, they have better things on their minds than feeding. Despite carp visibly swimming all around us for hours, we didn't manage any bites for a while. I tried to convince them to move to my other spot after a few hours, but the dad insisted that the carp would eventually bite. Finally, after 5 hours or so, the first rod went off. The dad grabbed it, and started trying to fight the carp. Being old and very frail, he nearly got pulled into the river. Again, his devoted son stepped in, crouched down in front of his dad, and had him lean on him, sort of using his back as a rod holder, while holding the portable oxygen tank in the other hand. I held onto his dad to keep him standing.

By the time small carp was landed, his dad was completely out of breath, and need a while to recover. I wondered what would happen if we hooked into a bigger one. Sure enough, we got another run after about half hour, as carp often turn on to feed in bunches. This time, the father knew that the fish was bigger than he could handle, so he let his son fight it after getting exhausted again. After landing it, he said they were done, so his son carried him back up to the car after saying our goodbyes. When he came down to pay for the outing, the one rod I still had going went off, and he proceeded to land the biggest carp of the day as a bonus.

My point to bringing up this story, was the outstanding display of respect and devotion that this individual had for his father. While respecting one's parent is a foremost commandment in many religions and cultures, it is rare to witness this sort of level.

The Talmud mentions the classic example of Esav's (Esau) level of respect for his father Isaac, being one of the strongest in known history. Despite Esav being less than righteous in many ways, this is the one area where he excelled more than others. As we believe that some European nations descended from Esav, I found it fitting that this person had that tremendous level of respect for his aging dad.

While most of my guided outings were positive experiences, there were a few that went in the other direction. Most of the people in our community are well aware that I'm an avid angler, and that I take people on guided outings every now and then. While some have hired me to do so, there are others, typically people I'm friendlier with, that ask for invitations. In general, I'm picky about who I invite to fish with me, and generally speaking, most people I end up inviting on a spur of the moment, can't (or won't) drop everything to go fishing. If they do, they will at least offer to pay for my gas if we were using my car to get there, as well as offer food, coffee, beer, etc.

For this following tale, I've changed the names of the people involved. "Nimrod" was a recent immigrant from Israel, looking to move to Canada permanently. He had started attending the synagogue where I normally go to pray on Shabbat. After finding out that I fish often, he got very insistent about inviting himself along to fish with me. Something about his attitude towards sport fishing rubbed me the wrong way. He seem very adamant about not wanting to spend a few bucks for a fishing license, and didn't believe in the idea of releasing fish. In a few short conversations with him, I tried to explain the reasoning behind these rules and practices, and consequences of not following. He seemed pretty stubborn in his mindset, so my gut feeling was not to invite him along.

One particular summer day, I had an outing planned with my older son. Back in the day, I didn't own a car, as I rarely needed one. A few times a month, I'd rent a car for about $20 per day, and combine some errands and fishing once I had the car. My son had to cancel at the last minute, but I was determined not to let the day and car rental "go to waste". Sure enough, as I'm loading the car, Nimrod walks by and sees me packing up my gear. He then proceeds to try to invite himself along as I imagined he would. Figuring that I'd finally get him off my back, I offered to take him provided he got a fishing license on the way, and suggested that he chip in for gas and the car rental fee, which he agreed to do. I asked myself, "How bad could it be"?

As we started driving to my spot a bit over an hour away, he called his cel phone provider to try to fight one of the charges he felt was unfair. It was a matter of a few dollars, literally pocket change, but when they refused, he got angry at them and kept asking to speak to a supervisor, getting louder all along. This went on for the entire hour it took us to get to the bait shop where we were to get him his license. After filling out the forms and getting his license, he proceeds to tell the clerk that he has no cash or credit card to pay for the license. At which point I offer to pay the whopping $11, after he promised to refund me on the way home.

After an annoying start to my day, I got the rods set up, and sure enough, Nimrod landed his first carp, with a bit of my help. When I suggested that we release it, he got very adamant about wanting to keep it for a friend. Having a keepnet on hand, I figured we can keep it alive until he figured out who to give it to. As the day went on, he made a few phone calls to friends of his, but no takers for the carp as far as I could tell. During which time we added 2 more carp to the keepnet.

Finally, we landed a big channel catfish. As catfish are not kosher, frum Jews won't eat them. As such, I tell him we are going to release it in good shape. To my shock, Nimrod says he'd rather kill the catfish than release it, simply because he found it ugly. With enough of this absurdity, I released the catfish and called it a day. In the meanwhile, he said he had found someone that wanted the carp, so I killed and bagged them for the ride home.

Shortly before getting home, we stopped at a bank machine, Nimrod comes back with $20 for me, telling me that his account is empty, and that he has no more money. At least it covered the money I lent him for his fishing license, but the rest barely covered half the gas cost at best. He then asked me to stop by his friend's house to deliver the 3 carp we harvested. Turns out that I knew his friend well. Moe (not his real name) frequently attended the same synagogue I did, and I'd known him for many years. After parking nearby, Nimrod delivers the carp, rings his bell, and comes running back to the car asking me to drive. Turns out, Moe was never the least bit interested in any carp, they ended up in the garbage. Then Moe kept reminding me of the story every time I saw him, until he moved away a few years later. One of my more annoying outings, but at least I got another story to tell, after all was said and done.

In time, I realized that the spot I kept fishing for carp was a great numbers spot, but less of a trophy spot. Out of close to a thousand carp landed there, only a few reached the magical 30 lbs mark. I decided to seek out other spots with bigger sized carp, closer to home. After finding a few decent spots, I started tinkering with pre-baiting them before fishing, as they were close enough to home to make it worth my time.

Pre-baiting took my trophy carp fishing to an entirely different level. Not only was I able to target spots with bigger carp, but after few days of successful baiting, they would be waiting for me when I arrived, often biting shortly after getting my line in the water.

Eventually, it was only a matter of time until I found my best trophy spot. Funny enough, it was adjacent to a spot I had first fished for walleye on ice, and more specifically, I came across the exact spot while casting a big Topraider for musky from shore one summer evening. Never did I connect with any muskies there, but a number of factors made me decide to pre-bait the spot. Sure enough, my first few carp landed there were mostly over 25 lbs, some close to 30 lbs.

By the following season, I was hooking into 30 lbs carp there, and managed my biggest carp ever in the spring of 2021, which weighed just over 41 lbs!

By then, the dozens of outings I had done with paying customers had allowed me to afford the Euro gear I had once laughed off as being overkill. I still have a good 10 or so carp rods, along with matching baitrunner reals, a couple rods pods, bite alarms, bank sticks, specialized landing nets, etc.

I spend quite a bit of time still fishing for carp every season. Chasing carp is trophy fishing, meaning that most often, I'm sacrificing numbers for size. All those hours spent sitting around and waiting in between bites, become spiritually meaningful if spent learning or in prayer. I can't tell you how many tractates of the Talmud I've been able to go through sitting by a calm lake or river bank, but I'd safely guess the number of hours are in the hundreds. On days where my head isn't into it, or is saturated, a Tehillim (book of Psalms) is another option. With little to no distractions besides for the occasional bite alarm going off, and the ensuing carp battle, it would be hard to find a better suited place to enjoy learning, in a peaceful, relaxed setting.

Hours spent carping from shore can make for a lot of learning.

One such outing comes to mind. It was back in the spring of 2019, when I was mourning for my late father obm. I was fishing a small pond not far from home for carp, while learning Bava batra in His memory. I came across a discussion related to fishing laws, which would probably fall under etiquette in modern times.

To quote page 21B:

If a fisherman discovered the lair of a particular fish, and spread his net between that fish and it's lair, other fishermen must distance their nets from the fish, as far as the fish swims in one spell, up to one "parsah" (equivalent to 2.5 - 3 miles). Even though the first fisherman has not yet acquired the fish, he can prevent other fishermen from taking it. Once fish set their sights on food, they will certainly swim to it. Therefore, if a fisherman sets a trap with food near the lair of a fish, the fish is viewed as if it were already in his hands, If another fisherman would then take the fish, that would be tantamount to taking it directly from that fisherman (theft).

Evidently, talmudic law would have something to say about modern days "googans" (aka spot thieves), especially ones fishing a spot pre-baited by someone else.

Equally interesting to me as a carper, is the fact that people were prebaiting for thousands of years, as in all likelihood, the fish referred to in the talmudic passage were probably carp. Much of the talmud was compiled in the Galilee, where the only bodies of water are the Kinneret (Sea of Galilee) and Jordan River, and native species of kosher fish big enough to fight over, were likely carp.

Another, more recent outing reminded me of one of the childhood story books I used to read. I set up for a morning of carping, and started learning. About 1 hour in, I'm learning the story of Yossef mokir shabbat

THE CARP CRAZE

(shabbat 119a), . For those of you not familiar with it, the story goes as follows:

Yossef was a man living in Talmudic times, who spent whatever he had to honor the Shabbat every week. No matter what the cost, he'd purchase the finest foods possible in honor of the Shabbat meals. For this reason, he was given the moniker, "mokir Shabbat" (who treasures Shabbat).

One night, a rich person has a dream, in which he is told that all his wealth will end up going to Yossef. The next day, the rich man's advisors came up with a plan to thwart the dream. They advised him to liquidate his assets and invest into a big diamond that would be a lot easier to safeguard. The rich man followed their advice, bought the diamond, and sewed it into his hat, so it remained on him at all times. One day, the man is crossing a bridge, when a strong gust of wind blows his hat into the river. Eventually, the hat comes apart in the current, and a big fish gobbles up the diamond.

That Friday, a local fisherman catches an enormous fish. He comes to the market shortly before the start of Shabbat, with very little hope of selling such a big fish so close to the start of Shabbat. One of his friends advises him to go to Yossef, who was known for spending lavishly on shabbat. Sure enough, Yossef agrees to buy the fish, and when he guts it, the big diamond pops out, and Yossef was now rich beyond his dreams.

The cover of this story book (kids version) we used to read growing up, was illustrated with Yossef holding up a huge carp. Sure enough, within minutes of reading this in the Talmud, my line goes off, and I land my biggest carp of the season, over 36 lbs! Timing couldn't have been better. And no, I didn't gut it to check for diamonds, released her in good health instead.

Non anglers that see me catching big carp or see the pictures, are often amazed that I don't keep fish that big for the table. Especially people that come from cultures where catch and release is unheard of. Without trying to sound racist or prejudging anyone or race in particular, it's no big secret that many Asians, and Chinese immigrants in particular, are more prone to keeping whatever they catch, than any other group I've come across.

I always wondered why they would go through that much trouble. It wasn't until a few hands-on experiences guiding them for carp, that I began to understand a bit more.

While I encountered many Chinese families keeping basket loads of panfish, most of them weren't geared up for carp. One day, I caught this very odd looking carp in close proximity to a bike trail. I wanted a picture of the strange looking carp, but as I was alone, I figured I'd stop the first passerby and ask them to get a picture of me with the fish. Sure enough, an elderly Chinese man passed by on his bike, with a small bag of groceries hanging from the handlebars. He seemed fascinated by the decent 20 lbs carp, but unfortunately, didn't speak any English or French. After he took the picture, I was going to release the carp, but he motioned to me that he wanted to eat it. Fine by me. He proceeded to pull out a rope from his bag, pull it through the gills of the carp to hang it from his handlebars, and pedaled off with the live carp dangling in front of him! I still kick myself for not getting a picture of him.

My next experience came when I had a nice sized Chinese family hire me to take them carping. I mentioned that there were no bag limits on carp, but suggested that we release any over 15 lbs, as I prefer to selectively harvest smaller fish. On the day of the outing, they showed up in a Mercedes SUV, and mentioned that both the husband and wife were university teachers. They had a couple teenage kids, and brought along the grandfather, and old school immigrant that didn't speak a word of English.

Fishing started off quite well, they landed 4-5 carp within the first few hours. I was starting to wonder if they were planning on releasing any, so out of curiosity, I asked them how much place they had in their freezer. Seems they planned to keep whatever we caught, and give the excess fish away to their friends. At some point, one of the kids landed a bigger fish, probably over 15 lbs. I suggested that it may be a good candidate for live release, and the kid seemed excited to do so. Just as he was about to release it, the grandfather came with his garbage bag, indicating that he planned to harvest it. After a short argument between them, the kid acquiesced, but his father was quite unhappy with the disrespect he had shown his elder. They ended up harvesting 8 or 9 carp that day, God only knows how long it took them to clean them all, and it wasn't like they couldn't afford to buy fish. At that point, I told myself that there must be more to them keeping fish than I understand. I guessed it was cultural.

My next customers from China, were here on a Canada wide visit. The woman that hired me had been a student in Canada at some point, and she had returned home a couple years prior. She brought her parents and fiancé back on a Canada wide trip, and the activity they chose for their portion of the stay in Montreal, was to go fishing. Acting as a translator between myself and her family, I learned about how tough it was to catch wild fish in China. For the most part, every waterway is highly pressured, overfished, and probably polluted. People can spend a month fishing before catching anything, and most wild fish are very small. Many people there opt to fish stocked ponds, where they pay for the fish they catch by the centimeter. That sort of gave me a bit more insight on why they might revere catching wild fish.

The final episode to this story, was another father daughter trip I did back in October of 2018. Again, it was a Chinese foreign student who booked me to guide her dad for carp. He was visiting from Guangdong, and mentioned that he fishes for carp, almost on a daily basis. Unfortunately for him, the carp in his region of China rarely exceed 2 lbs, so I was confident enough that he would land a new PB. Again, they had mentioned wanting to keep the carp. Being that they had no car, I met them at Metro (subway) station near my home, and suggested that they bring along a cooler or big waterproof bin to put any carp into for the ride home. They brought along a nice size clear plastic bin.

Fishing was on and off, which is typical for a cold October day. He started off by landing a small carp in the 11-12 lbs range, to which he was already quite stoked. I kept it alive in a keepnet for him, figuring we'd have the option of keeping our catch as fresh as possible until the end of the day, and cull any bigger ones if need be. He seemed to be very intent on baiting and casting my rods, something which he was not used to at all, as I was using 12 foot carp rods, which require different casting technique. I eventually taught him how to do it through the day, and he finally hooked up a nice carp on one of the rods he set.

After a good fight with the big carp, we finally had it in the landing net, and he was literally jumping for joy, thanking me over and over gain in Chinese (his daughter was translating). After weighing the carp at 23 lbs, I suggested we release the fish, much to his shock. He almost seemed offended. I had his daughter explain the concept of selective harvest to him, but nothing doing. He really wanted to keep the fish, so I put it into the keepnet along with the smaller carp.

At this point, I was trying to gauge how they planned on cleaning the carp, as all they had were kitchen knives at home. They said they would be fine. By days end, I killed the first smaller carp for him, but when it came to the bigger one, he insisted on wanting to kill it himself. Seemed like an honor thing, of him killing the biggest fish he'd ever caught in his life.

We placed the 2 carp in the big bin. On the way home, I mentioned a fish store next to the metro station that may willing to clean them for a small fee, but again, they refused. Funny enough, they ended up taking the carp home by metro. I can only picture the horror of the other passengers in the crowded metro car with a huge bin with 2 visible dead carp in a couple inches of blood. Again, one of those moments I would have liked to get on camera.

All this, to just point out that there are cultural differences beyond what we may assume, when it comes to catch and release mentality.

Many individuals from various ethnic backgrounds have kept carp we caught in the past. Most of them have their specific recipes and ways of preparing carp for the table. Some eviscerate and salt the carp right away, others soak them for a couple days in a strong marinade. Some smoke them and others grind/mince them with garlic and onions to make burger like patties. The common denominator seems to be the fact that these recipes all try to mask the unpleasant fishy flavor of carp, at least when compared to some of the other local species of wild caught game fish we tend to eat more often, like perch, walleye, trout, crappie, bass and pike.

At this point, I feel it would be appropriate to mention another ritual in the Jewish calendar, named kapparot. On the eve of Yom Kippur (day of atonement), many Jews have the custom of symbolically transferring sins to either a live animal, or to give extra charity. In the case of live animals, the animal is killed after a short prayer is recited, and either eaten of given to the poor that can't afford a meal. Most often, chickens are used. Since chickens require ritual slaughter by a trained expert, the ritual typically takes place at the slaughterhouse. For those with no access to slaughterhouses or live chickens, many use live fish instead. Fish don't require slaughter, anyone can catch or purchase a live fish and dispatch it in any manner, once the ritual prayer has been recited.

My late grandfather had the custom of buying 2 live carp for the occasion every year, one for himself and one for my late grandmother. Being immigrants from Hungary and having survived the holocaust, carp were a delicacy to them. The live carp were kept in the bath tub the night before, and early in the morning, they would do the kapparot ritual, after which my grandmother would clean the carp and cook them into some sort of stew, to be eaten before the fast. As my kids grew up, at some point in time, I decided to revive the custom of using fish instead of the chickens I was used to. My kids much preferred taking the day off school to go fishing, instead of getting up before sunrise to go to a smelly slaughterhouse. For a good number of years, we alternated between going carp fishing and harvesting some carp for our neighbours. During other years, we went fishing for trout instead, and consumed them throughout the ensuing holidays. We still go every now and then, depending on the year.

On my end, I'm not a fan of eating carp. I tried a few recipes many years ago, and then more recently, in 2023, I kept a small carp, with the goal of properly deboning it, and cooking it into something palatable. Mission accomplished, though I only ended up with about 1 lb of boneless meat from a 9 lbs carp. I ended up putting some on the log fire BBQ, and some deep fried in bread crumbs, schnitzel style. Though I wouldn't bother trying it again, everyone that tasted it, said it was OK enough for them to eat.

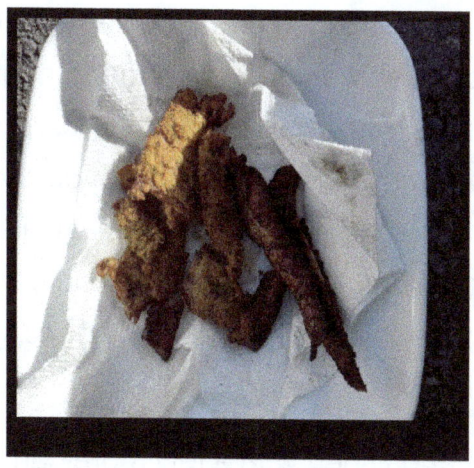

Suffice to say, I'll stick with releasing carp, especially the big trophy sized ones, which are most often egg laden females. Catching fish this big, using minimal amount of gear and investment, along with the convenience of driving to spots near my home, casting my line from shore, and catching up on my learning/reading while waiting for them to bite, is truly something unique. In today's world of fancy gear, big boats that require a mortgage, and the endless flow of new technologies "required" to be successful for many other species we fish for, these carp fill a niche.

Having been one of the first few Quebec born anglers to fish for carp here, I watched this niche evolve, almost from the beginning. Back before I caught my first carp, the few people targeting carp in Quebec, were a small handful of Europeans from various countries. Eventually, a couple of them put up a web site dedicated to carp fishing, along with an online forum. During the same time period, one of the biggest fishing forums in the province, was running a year long friendly tournament, based on accumulating points for various species caught. I was a member of both forums, and eventually, took some of the guys participating in the tournament out to get their first carp. Some of the forums members had a large following of fans they fished with, as well as on social media. Around 2011, two of these guys met up with an old Hungarian carp expert, and ended up shooting a lot of footage of their first few carp outings. Almost immediately, carp fishing blew up in Quebec, going from a tiny community of maybe a couple dozen carpers province wide, to hundreds. They were instrumental and having some of the bigger fishing stores bring in basic carp gear, though that didn't last too long. Today, we're mainly back to getting gear from a few specialized online based carp shops.

Though I've met and fished with a few more carpers since then, I still mainly fish for carp on my own, or with family / close friends.

Yesteryear carping with my little ones.

CHAPTER 4

Ice fishing

My love for ice fishing started off as a byproduct of our long winters. Not being able to fish for up to 5 months at a time, started to wear on my nerves, so at some point, my brother and I decided to give ice fishing a try.

Not owning any ice gear, nor knowing what to expect, we decided to go to an outfitter to ice fish for stocked trout. Lines, hole drilling, and a heated cabin were included in the plan, so all we needed to do was show up to fish. The previous winter, my brother had tried ice fishing for tomcods on the Ste Anne River at La Perade. He wasn't interested in going back there to catch loads of minnow sized fish that don't put up any sort of fight. However, he assumed that we'd be in the same sort of heated cabins on our trout trip.

We got to the lake bright and early. After checking in, one of the employees hauled us out to our cabin on a snowmobile. We got the feeling that he was looking at us a bit strangely, and soon enough, we figured out why. Based on my brother's past experience, he had incorrectly assumed that we would be fishing from the inside of our heated cabin. In reality, the cabin was just a place to stay warm, and all the fishing was done outside. Luckily for me, I had dressed a lot warmer than my brother, who was wearing a baseball cap and light jacket. With the temperature in the -20 range, he spent much of that day inside the cabin, watching the rudimentary "brimbale" type lines from the window. I was better off with my warmer clothing, and actually iced a trout on my first drop, using a small jig baited with live worm.

We eventually started returning there once or twice every winter, and figuring out new tricks and tactics on how to target these trout. In hindsight, we knew very little about ice fishing back them, and over the years, after many outings both with our kids and customers, we've come a very long way, to say the least.

Some of our first ice fishing trips to Pourvoirie Baroux, early 2000's.

These days, I'm not much of a fan of fishing these put and take style ponds or small lakes, that often get stocked while we are there fishing. After the first couple seasons of ice fishing only this style, I went out for my first "real" ice fishing experience, targeting pike and perch with my friend Mike, out on public land. He had the gear and a lot of ice fishing experience, and I gained a lot of insight from him.

Mike with pike.

Soon enough, I decided to dedicate some extra time to ice fishing. I started by getting a hand auger, and doing a fair bit of exploring on various lakes and rivers within an hour or so from Montreal. Most of what I caught back then were panfish, just blind jigging under ice. Eventually, I splurged a bit, and bought myself a Humminbird ice flasher. Basically, a real time live sonar of sorts, that upped my ice jigging game to the next level.

Besides for being able to target schools of fish, I was now able to pattern what the fish were more prone to bite, as far as lures, cadence, suspended depths, etc. Basically, and entire new world opened up under the ice, and chasing bigger predators now came into play as well. Various ice fishing styles exist, and each person might have their preferences. Most people that I encounter on the ice, favor the use of shelters. Some have dedicated shanties, but most use popup style shelters that give them a bit more freedom to move around. All use some type of heaters, usually log fires in cabins or shanties, or portable heaters in popup shelters.

I gave up on the shelter I once bought, after my first (and only) outing with it.

I no longer use any type of shelters when ice fishing. I prefer to fish out in the open, and keep warm by constantly moving and drilling more holes. If find that it makes fishing more exciting, and also provides a great day of exercise, as opposed to being stationary sitting around all day, while drinking beer in a heated shelter.

Towing a sled on foot is perfect for run n gun style ice fishing.

I actually enjoy drilling, whether using a manual ice auger, or more recently, my Ion G2 electric auger. Moving around on a given waterbody, I map out various depths, knowing where I achieved success in the past, while gaining valuable information, which often carries over to open water fishing in the summer.

Occasionally, I'll choose to still fish on ice using tip up (flag) lines. Being allowed to use up to 10 lines in some zones of Quebec, allows a nice spread of lines, and various options for bait. Most of the time, Northern pike are the target species, with a possible shot at a rare musky on some waterways. Ever since the live bait ban in 2017, my bait of choice is either frozen mackerels or frozen smelt. These are easy to come by in most grocery stores, and for the most part, they leave a stronger scent trail in the water than minnows. They come in bigger sizes too. More recently, I've had some success using big hot dogs for bait as well. That being said, I've also fished for carp on ice using similar tactics, but using boilies as bait.

As opposed to my run and gun style of drilling when jigging on ice, setting tip up lines is a lot more sedentary. As such, one tends to get cold a lot faster, so in these cases, I prefer to either stay on shore or on ice in a heated vehicle, waiting for flags to spring up.

A nice meter long Northern pike, Ari's biggest on ice to date.

Fishing from a heated car is ideal for those that don't enjoy the cold.

For me, ice fishing is the great equalizer. Between no longer owning a boat, and many waterways where launching a boat is difficult to impossible, the hardwater season is my shot at being on equal footing with anyone else, on lakes, and even in regions where I don't fish during the open water season. Granted, ice fishing is far from open water fishing, as it's basically impossible to cover anywhere near the same amount of water. However, certain species lend themselves to being caught on ice, just as well, if not better than in open water. Lake trout and perch come to mind.

Non anglers are generally fascinated about the idea of ice fishing, especially when they hear that I do it out in the open most of the time. Wild misconceptions about it being extremely dangerous, to being extremely cold. While both can be true to a novice, with a little experience and some common sense, ice fishing is a lot safer than other winter activities like skiing, ice skating, tobogganing, and snowmobile riding, to name a few.

First, one needs to make sure to be properly dressed. Most important, is to have very warm insulated boots, that are 100% waterproof all the way to the top, preferably as close to the knee as possible. A good pair of thermal socks under them is even better. I can't stress the importance of this enough. Cold or wet feet will ruin an outing in minutes, and walking around in a few inches of wet snow or slush will test and expose unsuitable footwear in no time.

Next, thermal undergarments as a base layer, preferably the thicker style (not athletic spandex). Add a normal layer of clothing, heavy sweatshirt or hoodie. For outer layer, bib style snowpants, preferably waterproof, or at least water resistant. A heavy parka with big hood, and lot's of inner and outer pockets. A tuque style winter hat under the hood, or possibly even a ski mask on very cold day, and last but not least, a very warm pair of mittens.

Personally, my hands rarely get cold, unless I'm fishing in extremely cold wind chills, but having a hand towel nearby is useful to get your hands dry after handling fish, as long as it doesn't freeze.

Next step in safety, is the use of a spud bar. While not too important for much of the ice season, it is likely the most important tool to have with you at early ice, or late ice. While most small lakes and ponds freeze somewhat evenly, there is always a chance of thinner ice due to warmer underwater current, or feeder creeks closer to shore. Hitting the ice at every step or two, is the only way to proceed, until you can determine the ice to be safe enough in your immediate area. I prefer solid ice at least 3.5 inches thick, but will occasionally venture out onto 3 inches on smaller ponds. I've seen people out on less ice than that, but for me, it's simply too nerve racking to be able to enjoy my outing unless I'm standing on my bare minimum. Once I'm on 4 inches all around, I generally don't bother with the spud bar, and just keep checking the ice thickness with every hole I drill.

Something that takes quite a bit of getting used to is cracking ice. This often occurs when the ice is expanding as it gets colder, especially after a warm spell, or rain. As the ice expands, it creates a lot of pressure, eventually cracking with loud "explosions", which can actually be felt. Drilling a hole into ice that is under pressure, will often create a boom and resulting cracks underfoot. While this is quite scary at first, it's very commonplace, and you get used to it, as best possible.

A number of years ago, my son and I were fishing a deep lake, where over time, I've probably experienced the most violent cracking, to the point where the ice vibrates hard enough to cause waves under the surface, which occasionally shoot water up through my ice holes. Before this particular outing, a student in a local university had contacted me about tagging along to take some pictures and video for his school project. I accepted, and he met us at the parking spot near the lake. I warned him about the probability of cracking ice, and told him to "just ignore it", and that refreezing ice was just getting safer. Easier said than done. I saw him twitch every time he heard any slight crack, even far across the lake. At some point, he decided to film my son drilling a hole. Just as the auger pierced through the ice, there was a giant explosion from the released pressure, forming a huge crack right under their feet. The student literally jumped a few feet in the air, looked at me, said he was done, and going home. I told him to relax and come back, but he looked at me sadly and said: "You don't understand. I just crapped my pants"!

Back to our discussion about gear… Next item on the list, is a suitable auger for whatever style and species I'm after. For much of my ice fishing over the years, I used a 6 inch diameter Fin Bore 3 from Rapala. Lightweight, easy to drill, extremely durable, and blades are simple enough to swap out or sharpen if need be. Provides a decent workout in ice thicker than 15 or so inches, and I've routinely drilled 40 to 50 holes per day on thinner ice. A 6 inch hole is suitable for most panfish, bass, and walleye in the regions I fish. Bigger species like pike, musky or lake trout require bigger 8 inch holes. For those, I messed around with various models of hand augers, but each had their drawbacks. Finally, around 2020, I got myself an 8 inch Ion G2 electric auger. While quite expensive, the speed, power, and extremely light weight in comparison to older gas augers, make the Ion one of the top models used by most serious ice anglers today. Easy to haul over long distance, no need to break one's back carrying it around. No fumes, fuel spills, mixing oil, or issues starting up in cold weather, pull start, choke, etc. I always carry spare cutters to match the auger I'm using, as well as the proper wrench to switch them out with, if need be.

For lines, lures, and bait, my selection will vary depending on the style(s) I choose to fish on a given outing. Assuming I'm going to stick with jigging, I'll usually keep 2 ice rods rigged, one with a tiny spoon or jigging rap, the other with a small lipless rattle bait. Most often, I'll tip one or both trebles with a live mealworm, which are hardy, relatively cheap, and easy to find in many pet shops. I like to use fluorocarbon line in winter, as it's less visible to fish, but more importantly, doesn't get waterlogged and freeze up like braided lines do. 6 to 8 lbs test works well for most of the lures I use.

The use of a flasher type sonar becomes quite important when jigging on ice. While various models exist, from very basic to crazy fancy, they all serve the same purpose. Namely, the ability to view the depth, your lure being jigged in real time, and the way fish are reacting to what you are doing. Ultimately, this will dictate your course of action, often for much of your outing.

In general, my preference is to give a new ice hole about 5 minutes or so to produce results. If it doesn't, I'll drill a new hole 20 to 50 feet away, depending on the size of the waterbody I'm fishing on, or on how much water I plan to cover. I'll alternate between 3-4 lures when things are quiet, but usually, 1-2 lures will be enough. When I finally find fish, I'll try to pattern the depth and cadence that triggered each bite, and then attempt to replicate that on subsequent holes drilled. I can easily fish 40 to 50 holes in a day, unless I hit some really big schools of fish that keep me fishing a given hole for longer.

The exception to this system, is when I fish stationary tip up lines. In those cases, I'll set up my limit of allowed lines minus 1. I'll bait them using disposable gloves, as mackerel and smelt have quite a strong smell. I'll then jig a lure using an ice rod with my last legal line, staying close enough to my tip ups to be able to get to the line on time when a fish hits.

Over the years, I've been quite surprised time and time again, by the size or numbers of many of the catches I've enjoyed on ice. For example, 2 of my 3 biggest largemouth bass were caught on ice, something that completely defies logic. Largemouth bass are a warm water species, with Southern Canada being the northernmost part of their range. The widely shut down under ice, often remaining suspended close to bottom near the deeper part of the given lakes or rivers I catch them in. I believe most bites are reaction strikes, as when I've kept some in the winter, their stomachs were usually empty. The fact that I've caught so many more largemouth bass in open water, including some pretty big ones, makes it even more wondrous that my biggest bass ever was caught on ice, and that both of my biggest ice bass were caught on relatively tiny waterways.

I've also landed most of my jumbo perch on ice, as well as having lost the biggest walleye I've ever hooked right at the hole, and a monstrous pike as well. Both of those fish still haunt me years later.

Sometimes, the biggest specimens are in the smallest ponds.

Another amazing benefit to ice fishing, is the ability to target hard to access, pristine lakes, with little to no pollution. This makes for just about the cleanest, healthiest and freshest fish one can find. Leaving a fish on ice all day, I can drive home a couple hours, and they'll actually come back to life when I thaw them before filleting, provided they didn't freeze solid. A large percentage of the fish I keep for my freezer, come from the few months that I target them on ice. Mostly, it's the only time I'll target tasty panfish like perch and crappie. You simply can't get fresher fish anywhere.

A tasty afternoon's catch.

Unfortunately, as with many other types of fishing, good spots come and go for various reasons. Natural fish kills, overfishing, loss of access to spots by either privatization or loss of suitable parking, and regulation changes, just to name a few. This keeps a delicate balance between returning to spots year after year hoping to match more successful days from the past, to putting in the time and effort to trying new spots. When choosing the latter, I always have the same couple concepts as my mindset: First, I won't catch anything unless I'm on the water, fishing. Next, If I'm not discovering a new hot spot, I'm eliminating a bad one.

Even when my time and effort don't necessarily pay off at first, there can be quite rewarding dividends down the line. Here are couple cases to illustrate the point...

Back around 2015, I ice fished a spot on the St Lawrence River not far from Montreal for the first time. With plenty of parking nearby and easy access to the water, it made for a nice afternoon outing. My target species was walleye, and while I was lucky to get on a decent evening bite, they were all very small. Over the next couple winters, ice fishing at the spot got tougher, to where it simply wasn't worth much time and effort to go there anymore. On a particular spring day, long after the ice was one, a carp customer of mine wanted to stay closer to Montreal, rather than further away, where I normally take most of my customers to fish for carp. I took their group to shore fish for carp at my ice fishing spot, and sure enough, they landed some big ones. During a similar situation with another group of customers the following spring, the same thing happened, except that these carp were even bigger, with a couple weighing in the mid thirties. Needless to say, I stumbled onto a great carp fishing spot thanks to ice fishing. Not only do I still fish there today, but I've caught my biggest carp ever there, as well as the highest percentage of trophy sized carp when compared to any other spots I fish for them, by a long shot.

A chunky common carp caught near a spot I found on ice.

Another similar story occurred more recently. In 2021, my son Ari and I decided to try a small lake in the Outaouais region that gets stocked with brook trout every now and then. Unknown to us, it hadn't been stocked for a while due to the Covid pandemic. This forced us to do a lot of trekking and drilling in deep snow and thick ice, and all we managed to catch were a few tiny perch. I downsized my lure to a tiny jigging spoon just to get a bit more action and salvage

My first ice smallie.

what was left of our day. As I slowly made my way towards one of the shorelines drilling and fishing, I sent my lure down to the bottom in 27 feet of water. I got hit, and from the strong pull on my line, I thought I had finally hooked into a very nice trout. To my huge surprise, it ended being a solid 3.5 lbs smallmouth bass, my first ever on ice up until that point. The lake that I had just about written off my list, was now at the top of my list to try in summer from my float tube, and sure enough, I've had some of my best smallmouth bass fishing from the float tube on that lake in subsequent years, routinely pulling out smallies over 4 lbs. I never would have known about the lake if I hadn't ice fished it for trout, and never would have thought it had a decent population of huge smallies for its size, had I not had that "lucky" drop.

Of course, things can work just as well the other way. Case in point is a small lake I first fished from my float tube back in 2020. During my first solo outing there, I managed to hook close to 50 bass in a few hours, mainly smaller largemouth mixed in with a few smallmouth. Over the years, I returned there a number of times on ice, and have had some absolutely crazy days with insane ice action, including my highest number of bass caught on ice in a day. 30 Largemouth bass, 4 smallmouth bass and 23 perch, mainly jumbos over 10 inches were all landed during about 8 hours of solo ice fishing one spring.

This small lake I found while float tubing has produced hundreds of iced bass and perch.

All to illustrate the hand in hand relationship of open water fishing to ice fishing. Had I been needlessly worried about cold weather, unsafe ice, or any other detrimental excuse I've heard about ice fishing over the years, I'd have missed out on hundreds of days of great fishing, countless amounts of pristine, fresh fillets for the table, and some of the biggest and most memorable catches of panfish and bass I've encountered to date.

That being said, common sense must prevail when it comes to safety. No life is worth risking for a fish, even when that means forgoing the long drive one can make, only to find unsafe ice upon arrival. Better to be slightly annoyed, but safe to return after the next cold front.

There is something very spiritual about fishing out in the woods. Even more so in the dead quiet of winter. Seeing nature the way God created it, observing the eco system in harmony, without any man made structure, buildings, cars, or power lines, I often find myself in a heightened spiritual state of mind in that sort of setting. Many great Jewish scholars, leaders, and saints, would travel to secluded forests in order to practice something called "hitbodedut". This is the practice of direct verbal communication with God. As opposed to pre-scripted prayers that are recited in groups, hitbodedut is informal, and always done in private. The lack of distractions offered in a forest setting, are ideal conditions conducive to meaningful hitbodedut.

Mystical Judaism often alludes to elevating one's surroundings though the practice of prayer, and other positive commandments we follow. We believe that by reciting a prayer before eating, will on some level, spiritually elevate the food we are eating. Reciting a daily prayer, will similarly elevate the chalet, yard, or beach we are in (or on) at the time. Being able to travel to remote areas where few (if any) frum Jews have ever set foot before, there is something to be said about likely being the first Jewish prayer to be recited at a given spot. Reciting Shehakol and Borei nefashot (blessing before & after eating) on a fish I caught before eating it, also gives it significantly more meaning to the prayer, than if I were to simply have gone to the store to buy it.

There is something primordial about feeding fresh caught fish to your family in winter.

Last but not least, is the tale of a what seemingly may have ended up being just another fishing spot I stumbled onto, but turned being much more meaningful to me. After confirming that there were some decent carp in the small lake, I also found a good population of largemouth bass, as well as some pike, and big panfish.

I eventually fished there on ice a few times, managing some early season bass on thinner ice. Still wanting to explore many lakes in other regions during the winter, I didn't go back to this spot too often.

All that changed with the passing of my dear dad in February 2019. As a practicing Jewish mourner, it was my religious duty to pray with a quorum of 10+ men in a synagogue 3 times per day. Though I had typically done this every day up until that point, I often just did the prayers alone at some point during my fishing outings. As the prayer for departed souls can only be recited with 10 others praying along, I was no longer able to fish too far away from Montreal, and outings were going to be limited to a maximum of about 5 hours, in order for me to be able attend afternoon prayers in a group before sunset, which occurs quite early in the winter.

After the 7 day Shiva period (where we don't leave the house for 7 days), I was itching to get out again. Shiva ended on a bright sunny morning late in February 2019, and I headed straight to this spot to do some much needed fishing, hoping catching some more bass on ice. Sure enough, the small lake did not disappoint. I managed to ice more bass than ever before, up until that point. Even better than the fishing, I was able to find my own personal, peaceful, and quiet place to mourn my father's passing in my own special way. I imagined him looking down on me hauling bass after bass through the ice, something which he had never wanted to try during his lifetime. Over the next couple weeks, during the Shloshim (30 day) mourning period, I managed a few more miraculous bass outings.

Early in March of that year, I landed my biggest largemouth ever. It measured 22 inches, but I couldn't weigh it do to my scale being frozen. Regardless, hauling a beast that size out of a tiny lake through a 6 inch hole will remain engraved in my memory for years to come.

CHAPTER 5

Outfitters

For the most part, we frum Jews, tend to live in areas that have the infrastructure to facilitate our lives as observant Jews. We generally choose to live in walking distance of synagogues, where we pray with a quorum of at least 10 other Jewish men, 3 times a day. As we don't drive on Saturdays or during many other Jewish holidays, the need to have a synagogue in walking distance is a pre-requisite. Other aspects to consider, are access to kosher food, and Jewish schooling for our children. The majority of large Jewish communities around the world usually tend to be localized around this sort of infrastructure.

Much of my lifelong fishing adventures take me to remote places, where frum Jews are non existent. Quite often, the people I end up fishing with have never met a (practicing) Jew in their lives. Sadly, many of them may have preconceived notions about us, that are not always favorable. Not of their own faults, just a combination of being told something by someone that was ignorant, and without anyone there to refute what they heard, they may have assumed some truth to some of these "classic" tropes.

I often see myself as an ambassador of sorts, when it comes to showing these people, who we really are. Keeping our campground clean, tipping guides, being respectful of other cultures, and just generally showing them that I actually have a clue about what I'm talking about when it comes to our shared passions for fishing, go a very long way in repairing any potential negativity one may have had before meeting us.

Up until the end of 1990's, most of the fishing I did was on public land. The few short overnight trips we did were mainly to campgrounds that offered access to a given lake or river, usually public, and inhabited.

My first experience with outfitters was somewhere around 2000, when my brother and I tried ice fishing for stocked trout at an outfitter, though it was only a day trip. My first real experience staying at an outfitter was in 2002. We rented a small cabin on Lac Maloon, a relatively small lake, with an outfitter that had non exclusive rights. Meaning that others, including homeowners, had rights to access and fish the lake. The outfitter in question had arranged for periodical stocking of walleyes, and the lake had a decent smallmouth bass population. We did OK there during a couple outings.

A decent smallie from Lac Maloon.

Later that summer, my brother and I, along with our friend Raphy, decided to return there for a few days. We found out the cabins were all booked, so we decided to look elsewhere. Back in those days, the Federation des Pourvoiries du Quebec (Quebec outfitters federation or FPQ), put out a yearly booklet listing all outfitters by region. It contained details regarding each outfitters, such as the species of fish and game available there, numbers of cabins, pricing, and a small blurb about the outfitter, along with a few pictures.

We stumbled on Mijocama outfitter, which had opened a few years prior. Due to the proximity to Montreal, and affordable pricing, we decided to book a cabin there for a few days. It was our first experience living off the grid. Everything in the camp was propane powered, though they had temporary evening power when the camp's main generator turned on for a few hours around sunset.

Some catches from our first trip to Mijocama back in 2002.

The beauty of being out in virtually untouched nature was an eye opener for us. The wildlife we encountered, the peace and calm of quiet sunrises and sunsets, and the fresh smell of the deep woods, were compliments to the quality of bass fishing there at the time. We all caught largemouth bass there during that trip, something which we were very excited about. We resolved to return again the following summer, and when we did, we were a lot more educated regarding catching more and bigger bass.

Over the following years, my kids started joining us for the yearly trip to Mijocama for the bass opener. The sizes and numbers of our catches just kept getting better. Around 2005, my brother and I decided to bring along my late father, obm. Mijocama had just finished building their first luxury cabin, which boasted 2 floors, 2 bathrooms, full time electricity, and clean drinking water from its own well. Best of all, it was away from all the other cabins in the main camp, so we had a peace, quiet and privacy. As I mentioned in a previous chapter, my childhood friend Jimmy joined us for this trip, so he and I reunited there after not having fished together for close to two decades.

Over 20 years of trips (and counting) to Mijocama.with my kids.

The largemouth bass fishing was still off the charts back then, though the population of smallmouth bass in the lake had just about been wiped out, as often happens when largemouth bass are introduced. The pike fishing had started picking up a bit as well. The trip was a smashing success, and since then, we've been booking the same cabin every season around the same date.

Our growing family at Mijocama with Jocelyn (the owner).

At first, our group grew enough to fill all the cabins beds. I brought more kids along each year as they kept getting older, Jimmy brought along his boys and dad as well. Eventually, my old friend Albert joined us, and the following year, he brought along his son in law, Howard. By this point, our group had outgrown the cabin. Jimmy rented his own place in the main camp, as did Howard and Albert. Every morning, we'd gather at my cabin for morning prayers, as we now had the mandatory minimum of 10 men for our minyan (quorum).

Bonfires and fireworks became part of our Mijocama nightly ritual.

Mijocama has some of the region's biggest largemouth bass

Boating lessons were always a blast fore the kids.

We've done a few ice fishing trips to Mijocama as well.

Life went on. Eventually, my dad and Albert were getting too old for these trips, and the quality of fishing started dwindling. The dynamic changed a bit, as Jimmy had invited some of his friends and their teenage kids. Eventually, they rented a newer, even bigger luxury cabin, that fit 20 people. That lasted for a few seasons, until the owner sold the cabin off to a friend of his. At that point, Jimmy's large gang was now renting most of the waterfront cabins in the camp, and even then, they were on rotation, in order to accommodate the large number of friends coming up to hang out with them.

For the most part, Jimmy and I, along with my teenage kids were the diehard anglers, and most others were there more for the vacation, drinks, bbq's and bonfires. I met many new friends during these trips, spanning over a couple decades.

Hands down, Mijocama has to be the place where I have more fishing memories than anywhere else. From the early days of figuring out the lake with my brother and Ari as a young child, to all the great times with my growing family and late father, every turn, tree and log on the lake has some sort of story or moment captured in my mind.

While most of the fishing we have done at Mijocama took place on the main lake in the camp (Giles lake), they have some more remote lakes with difficult access, containing other species. Lac Roche was mostly the dedicated pike lake, Superior is stocked with brook and rainbow trout, and Chat is connected to Giles by a small feeder stream. Each have their own unique challenges.

Outside of our yearly trip for the bass opener, I've explored most of these lakes during other, smaller trips, either with my brother or with Jimmy. Not having the responsibility of younger kids to take care of and feed, I was able to dedicate full summer days to accessing and "beating up" these lakes. Though we had some good success on them, overall, the consensus has been to stick with Giles lake at the main camp. Having fished there for well over 100 days by now, I have a very good knowledge of the lake, although as everything else in nature, it keeps changing all the time.

The camp's owner, Jocelyn, spent a good deal of time showing people how to fillet bass and pike, and sort of encouraged them to keep some for the table. While I pretty much released all of my bass prior to going to Mijocama, my brother and I decided to keep our bag limits during one of our early trips there. We easily limited out on big 3-4 lb largies, mainly females. Over the next decade or so, we kept at it, using Giles lake as our yearly source of fresh fish, as did many of the other guests fishing at Mijocama all summer.

As a result, the largemouth bass numbers started to dwindle. At that point, I started practicing selective harvest, keeping a few smaller bass for the table, and releasing the bigger ones in good condition. Still, the damage had been done, and as a result, Northern pike seem to have taken over a lot of the biomass of predatory sport fish in the lake. In our earlier days there, it was not common to catch more than a pike or two during the entire trip, and to go through dozens of bass, with many big ones. That has now flipped, to where we have been catching more pike than bass recently, to the point where we've come home with multiple bag limits of pike and very few bass to show for.

Over the years, we have learned many lessons, and enjoyed and lived though a lifetime of good memories at Mijocama, simply too many to share. A few come to mind…

Back around 2004, I brought along my oldest son Ari, who was then 7 years old, along with my brother. It was our first time planning to keep bass for the table, so we brought along a stringer. We launched our boat on a Sunday morning, and our first spot was a smashing success. Within ½ hour or so, we had landed our first bag limit of 6 bass, mainly in the 2.5 to 4 lbs range. As we motored to our next spot, we came around a bend, and saw the owner Jocelyn, along with another customer on the shore. We idled to say hello, and when he asked us how it was going, I lifted the heavy stringer, probably close to 20 lbs of bass or so on it. Both their eyes nearly popped out of their sockets in amazement. As I later found out, the client had been there for a few days without catching anything, and was starting to doubt whether or not there were any bass in the lake. He would never have believed us catching a limit in our first

½ hour, had he not seen our stringer. A similar situation occurred, when I decided to cast off our dock one afternoon. Jocelyn was with a customer at a neighboring cabin. My first cast right up to shore, landed a good 17 inch bass, and again, they were both freaking out. When I innocently asked what the big deal was, I learned that this guy had been there for a week, without catching any bass, and here I just pulled a decent one of the shore in front of his eyes, a few meters from his cabin. Needless to say, Jocelyn and I have become friendly over the years.

In 2006, I returned to Mijocama in August with my brother David. Bass fishing was still OK, but we got onto our first crazy pike bite, with me landing a 35 inch pike, still the biggest one recorded from Giles lake to date. During that trip, we met a lady visiting from Texas. Seeing my Texas themed T-shirt, we got to talking a bit. Turns out, her family were the original owners of Giles lake, her lastname being Giles as well. She was visiting as part of researching her family history. We learned that they had lived in Texas back in the late 1800's, at which time the government of Canada was giving away remote chunks of land to anyone willing to settle there. They made the trip to Ottawa by train, and the rest by horse and buggy. At some point later in time, the family opened a fishing camp on Giles lake, and many of the original cabins in the main camp are still in use today. They were the ones that originally stocked largemouth bass into Giles lake, from where they eventually made their way into two of the smaller connecting lakes. To date, they remain the only lakes in the region to contain largemouth bass.

In the summer of 2008, we arrived at Mijocama for our annual family bass fishing trip. Upon arrival, Jocelyn mentioned that the FPQ was running a promotional contest, with some very nice prizes. The contest was set up per species, in categories of men, women and children. Basically, the biggest pike, walleye, bass and trout winners in each division, would be awarded $500 gift certificate in Le Baron Sport (fishing / hunting store, no longer in existence), a fly rod, and a trip to one of the 15 or so participating outfitters. Being that Mijocama is one of the only outfitters to have bass on their territory, we knew that the winners in each division were very likely to have caught the winning fish there. Sure enough, my son Avi, then 7 years old, was with me on our first evening out. I set out a big juicy worm under a popping cork style bobber, and when the line went under, he set on the big bass. Luckily, he was able to keep it pinned, and we landed a nice 18 inch bass, big enough to actually win the division. The FPQ sent us the gift certificate, and were somewhat dismayed that we had won a free bear hunting trip to Le Domaine Shannon, in addition to the other prizes. Being that we don't hunt, and that my kids were all in school during Quebec's bear season, I called the outfitter, who were happy to swap it for a walleye trip later the following summer.

Avi's winning bass for the FPQ contest.

Unfortunately for Avi, he wasn't ready for a trip as remote as Le Domaine Shannon, due to his young age, and, as he was scheduled to visit his grandparents in the USA with my wife, I took my older son Ari along for the trip instead of Avi.

Driving up to Le Domaine Shannon for the first time, was an experience still etched in my mind. We left late on a Saturday night, reaching the main forest road up to the outfitter at the crack of dawn. Within minutes on the road, a wolf came charging out of the woods running straight for the car. I had never seen one in the wild up until that point. A few minutes later, we noticed a small black bear crossing the road. Now I knew I was in more wild of a place that I had ever fished at. After checking in at the main camp, we still had a good 45 minute drive to Lac Lenotre, where we stayed in a remote, propane powered cabin. On the way there, I saw a very big cat crossing the secondary road, carrying a hare in its mouth. Turned out it was a very rare cougar, as I described it having a long tail and beige coat. I later found out that the province of Quebec has never officially accepted the presence of cougars here, despite many sightings over the past few decades.

More importantly, the fishing we enjoyed over the next few days was phenomenal. I easily caught my bag limit of 8 slot sized walleye. We returned to the main camp to purchase a license for Ari. Though he was allowed to fish under my license as a minor, the nominal $20 or so fee allowed us to take another bag limit. Over the next 2 days, we consumed walleyes until we couldn't any more, and despite that, we left with 2 bag limits, total of 16 walleyes.

My first morning at Le Domaine Shannon, August 2010.

On our way out, I came up with an idea. I had launched a web site a couple years prior (more on that in a future chapter), and after getting a decent amount of web traffic, I figured I'd offer to send the outfitter some customers in return for credits towards free fishing trips. To my delight, Serge (the owner) accepted my offer. Over the years, we have gone back to Le Domaine Shannon many times. Our deal still stands, with me sending them groups of clients on a regular basis, in exchange for weeklong trips to remote lakes on their exclusive territory.

Le Domanie Shannon has a nice mix of remote lakes to fish, which is always the option I choose. I prefer the peace and quiet of having an entire lake to ourselves, and without any phone, internet access, or even electricity, we can devote our trips to fishing and spending time with each other. Throughout the years, and many trips to Le Domaine Shannon, we have explored various lakes. To date, my favorite remains Lac Wahoo. Despite an abundance of very small pike, it does contain some very nice sized pike into the 20 lbs range. Though catching these pike is rare since the ban on dead bait, every cast still has the potential to land a new PB. Between myself and my sons, we have all landed our biggest pike on Lac Wahoo.

4 of my sons with some double digit pike from Lac Wahoo.

The lake also contains a decent walleye population, though it's extremely rare to catch one over 2 lbs there. The big exception to that was in 2020, my son Eli landed a monstrous 30 inch / 9 lbs walleye, by far the biggest ever landed on the lake since the Danis family purchased the outfitter back in the 1960's.

While bugs are horrendous in June and July, by mid August we can stay outdoors after dark.

Another aspect of travel related fishing, is access to kosher food, which is the strict set of dietary laws we follow. Inherently, many of the fish I target when travelling are kosher, so fresh fish becomes a staple part of our meal plans. I also bring along all my own food, as I wouldn't be able to eat food cooked at most fishing lodges. Pots, pans, grills, plates and cutlery, all need to be kosher as well, meaning that they haven't come into contact with food forbidden to us. As such, I bring along a small kitchen on my trips to outfitters, and kosherize the stove top burners upon arrival. We can then cook using our utensils.

Kosherizing the kitchen and bringing along our own utensils so we can eat like "mentchen".

Group prayer often becomes an issue as well. In general, the 3 daily prayers we say, ought to be in the company of at least 10 Jewish males over the age of 13. This quorum is called "minyan". When praying with a minyan, the group is able to complete certain prayers that can only be done as part of a group. When praying individually and with less than 10 men, these prayers are omitted. While this is permissible if need be, it is not ideal.

Luckily for us, most of our recent yearly trips to Mijocama have had 20+ frum Jews, so we've been enjoying the presence of our minyan for many years there. This comes in very handy when one is in mandatory 11 month mourning period, after the loss of a parent, God forbid. During that period, a special prayer said by the mourner for the departed soul, is recited a few times during each of the 3 daily prayers, and requires the presence of a minyan. Over the years, myself, as well as some of our group members, were unfortunately mourning during our trips, and the fact that we had our minyan made if able for them to come along on the trip.

Daily minyan for Shacharit (morning prayers) at Mijocama.

A large number of outfitters in the Laurentians and neighboring Lanaudiere regions of the province, offer exclusively stocked trout. As I previously mentioned, my first few ice fishing trips were for stocked trout at an outfitter in the Laurentians, Pourvouirie Baroux. After a few seasons, they decided to shut down their ice fishing operation, focusing on summer fishing and hunting. We were forced to look elsewhere, and tried a few outfitters within the same 2 hour driving distance from home.

Eventually, we stumbled on a place named Coin Lavigne. My older son Ari was studying in the US at the time, and he was home for New year's break. A few days prior to the new year 2012, we were set to go there to ice fish for the first time, but -20C temperature deterred us. As Ari was set to leave during the first week of January, we figured we'd wait until after New year's day. With our luck, the only available day we had was even colder, with the outer temp at -32C when we arrived early in the morning. Luckily, they had heated cabins available near the ice holes, and we managed to catch 2 bag limits of 10 trout each. By far, better than we had done at any other place ice fishing for stocked trout, so I started going back to coin Lavigne year after year, and also with some groups of local clients or tourists that wanted to try ice fishing for the first time.

My kids with a couple bags limits of trout at Coin Lavigne.

By then, I had adapted my tactics, bringing along my own auger and sonar, which made the fishing much more effective, informative, and productive. Eventually, Coin Lavigne bought another outfitter named Renard Bleu, and moved their ice fishing operations there, keeping Coin Lavigne as the center for their snowmobile relay.

Trout fishing at Coin Lavigne was not limited to ice fishing only. I've done a number of fall trips there with my younger ones, during which we were generally able to catch our bag limits each time. The small lake that offers day trips (Lac en Coeur) is simple enough to fish. Once trout are hitting on the troll at a given depth, it isn't uncommon to keep catching them at the same depth all day long. As long as my battery for the trolling motor has power, we're in the game, and typically, we catch our limit before the battery runs out of power.

Some nice rainbow trout caught trolling on Lac en Coeur.

With over 450 outfitters in Quebec, there is no shortage of options. That being said, there is something to returning to a familiar lake where memories were made over the years. Recently, I fished Giles Lake at Mijocama for the n-th time. Having gone there on a yearly basis for over 20 years, every tree stump, rock, and bay, is filled with memories of my sons when they were little kids, fishing with my late father, and discovering the lake with my brother back in the days where I knew barely nothing in comparison to what I know today. Ditto for Le Domaine Shannon. These memories keep me going back year after year.

CHAPTER 6

Online presence

Killing two birds with one stone is a saying often used to describe efficiency. For example, If I have a couple hours during which I want to get some exercise, but also want to fish, I can combine the two by either biking to my fishing spot, or going out on my float tube for a few hours.

As I previously mentioned, my online business has given me a schedule flexible enough to be able to set aside time to fish on a regular basis. Around 2006 or 2007, after having increasing success both at fishing, and also in the business of trying to rank web sites at the top of search engine results, I came to the realization that creating a fishing web site would have many benefits.

First, all fishing related expenses would be a corporate expense, translating into roughly a 20% tax break on gear, trips, etc. Next, I'd be able to claim the 15% provincial and federal taxes back for fishing related expenses. Add the travel expense for the use of a vehicle, and it's was basically a no brainer from that aspect. After double checking the legalities with my corporate accountant, I began working on the web site.

Web ranking back in those days was a lot simpler, and less competitive than it is now. Aside from using the knowledge we had from building various other web sites with good ranking, fishing in particular lent itself to some additional beneficial SEO (search engine optimization) practices simply not available to other business categories. For example, someone selling shoes online could never hope to convince a competing online shoe store to cross promote each other. In the world of fishing resources, pictures and videos, it's a different ball game. I was able to promote my web site through many resources otherwise not available to other facets of my business, by sharing links, posting pictures and videos, to many other fishing industry related web sites.

The plan worked like a charm. Soon enough, the site I created (www.freshwaterphil.com) , was ranking at the top of most search engine results relating to fishing around Montreal, as well as other niches like carp fishing in Canada, etc.

Once my initial goal was achieved, the traffic started pouring in. Many locals were very interested in fishing spots around town, or fishing guides. Tourists were interested in guides, and fishing trips. At this point, I decided to cover many of these niches by either monetization, or mutually beneficial agreements with guides and outfitters.

First, I created my Montreal shore fishing spots guide. It was an electronic document containing tips and tricks on how to fish 10 popular spots around Montreal, along with maps to each spot, parking and access information, tips on what one may use and the species to catch at each given spot. For the nominal fee of $15, I'd send the document by email, as well as answer follow up questions.

Next, I put up a page promoting a few local fishing guides for various sport fish species like bass, pike, walleye, musky and sturgeon. With these guides, instead of charging them a finder's fee for booked outings, we agreed that I'd promote them in exchange for being able to fish with them during their less busy times. To me, having the shot at fishing with top notch guides for each of the target species, was worth more than a possible fee I'd charge to do the same thing.

At the same time, I put myself down as the guide for carp, and was able to successfully guide many newbies and tourists to some great carping over the years, as well as being able to upgrade and stock up on gear. Shortly after that started working, I started offering ice fishing excursions as well.

Lastly, I set up a similar system with a few outfitters, where I'd earn credits towards fishing trips at their lakes or lodges.

As time went along, and more people visited my fishing site, the monetization mechanisms were able to generate enough income for me to be able to invest in new equipment, trips, and pay for the gas used to drive to all these destinations.

Funny enough, during my early teens, I hoped that I may somehow someday earn a living from sport fishing. As an observant Jew, I eventually came to the realization that it wasn't going to happen. Most tournaments are run over weekends, most customers want to fish on Saturdays, and working as a full time guide in remote fishing camps, isn't compatible with an observant Jew's lifestyle when it comes to schedule, kosher food, public prayer in groups, etc.

Now, I was able to help many new anglers out, as well as spend countless days on the water doing what I enjoy. I gained extremely valuable experience in regards to many aspects of sport fishing during that time, and fished with people from all over the globe, sharing experiences, etc. I wasn't earning a living from my web site, but the extra income funded my fishing addiction for many years.

Further down the line, I set up a blog site (www.montreal-fishing.com). This was where I logged details and pictures of many of my outings. Where the web site was only updated from time to time, the blog updates are a regular occurrence, to where it has a good 500 or so blog entries at the present time (and growing).

Additionally, I was a member of a few online fishing forums. These were web sites dedicated to providing their members with access to create or reply to discussions spanning various fishing related topics, post pics, videos, etc. Some were local to Quebec and in French, other were North America wide, but targeted to niches like carp or ice fishing. As well, I joined other localized fishing forums if I was planning to spend some time visiting different areas and fishing on my own, such as Texas and Colorado to mention a couple. These forums were very active before the massive social media takeover, and had many very helpful members that were akin to virtual fishing buddies. We were able to message each other, and I ended up meeting a few fishing buddies through the forums.

Sometime around 2010 or so, forum traffic started to slowly decline, likely due to a combination of factors. The younger crowds were more active on quicker / simpler social media sites like Facebook or Instagram, both of which allowed rapid sharing of pictures and videos, eventually in real time. A local fishing group could be created in minutes, at no cost. As well, the older forum crowds that remained loyal to their forums simply aged, died out, or found other pastimes.

While I never bothered with Instagram, I did participate in a few targeted Facebook groups for a few years, but eventually, just got bored of them. As I was sort of getting tired of guiding, I had little interest in cross posting my information to a multitude of groups on a regular basis, as some of the younger guides do these days. Too much effort and not enough reward for me. Rather spend that time on the water, with my family, or doing more productive things, than working to create content for social media companies without compensation.

While I do post some occasional pictures to Facebook or videos to Youtube, for the most part, the only forum I still use is www.iceshanty.com , which is obviously targeted to ice fishing. I believe it has to be the largest online group of die hard ice warriors in North America, and quite possibly on the planet.

Time will tell where the internet takes us as far as fishing goes, but from past experience, it can be a double edged sword. On the one hand, social media and forums provide a great resource for anyone looking for new fishing buddies, spots, or other information. On the flip side, I've seen quite a few fisheries literally destroyed, by people simply posting a trophy fish with noticeable landmarks in the background. Some top caliber anglers are careless when it comes to sharing good spots with the masses, and the old school mentality of keeping a good spot to yourself, seems to have been replaced by momentary gratification of bragging rights. They then wonder why "their" spots get burned out by overfishing.

More recently, I came up with the idea of my charity bounty fishing, as another way to give a bit more meaning to all the fishing I do. Basically, every fish I catch is logged into a monthly chart, and the totals based on species and sizes of fish are logged. At the end or the month or pre-determined period, the tally is added up to a monthly total in dollar value. Anyone willing to participate in the bounty can donate the total to a charity of their choice, and / or a predetermined one of my choice. Our current world filled with strife and negativity, can definitely use some positive, good deeds. For more information, visit: https://freshwaterphil.com/charity-bounty.cfm

לעלוי נשמת אהרן בן יהושע חיים ז"ל

CHAPTER 7

Travel

When travelling abroad to fish, destinations will vary as far as to what is available to match a frum lifestyle. Being that I find myself in Miami often enough, there are hundreds of synagogues stretching from South Beach to West Palm Beach, and a vast number of kosher restaurants and grocery stores. As well, most of the large chain stores like Walmart and Publix, carry a diverse selection of foods that are inherently kosher, and many are

Chabad of Fort Lauderdale, FL.

certified as well. I happened to be in the mourning period for my late father while visiting Florida in 2019, and was glad to have a synagogue in Fort Lauderdale close enough to where we stayed and fished, so I could make it to the minyan scheduled every morning and evening.

A few hours drive to the Western part of Florida on the Gulf of Mexico, and you're in a different world, when it comes to frum infrastructure. There weren't any operating synagogues during my visits there in 2016 and 2017, and we made due eating cereal with milk and peanut butter sandwiches for a couple days. At least we were able to enjoy a few beers. Prayers were inevitably said without a minyan. Again, depending on one's level of observance, there are those who wouldn't put themselves in the position of not having a minyan, but I routinely end up doing so if I'm too far away to make it back to synagogue on time.

Travelling to fish opens up new experiences, venues, and species that don't exist in our fishing regions. Whether it's during a vacation, business trip, or simply travelling to fish, infinite possibilities make it tough to choose on where to go, what species to target, and how to go about it. I seem to juggle between do it yourself style trips, to all out big game fishing with top notch guides, sometimes a mix of both.

While a quick day trip to the Adirondacks to fish for trout may fall into this category, I'm talking more about further destinations, for species not available anywhere in driving distance. If I find myself in any such given area for any period of time, my mindset will take me to some sort of exotic fishing experience.

Around 2010, I started visiting Dallas, Texas, every February. For four years, my older son Ari attended high school there, and my in laws live there as well. I now had access to open water in mid winter, and place to stay. All I needed was a rod, a Texas fishing license, and a plan.

A nice striped bass caught shore fishing on Lake Texoma.

I started off with the goal of catching carp in Texas, while at the same time hoping to land my first smallmouth buffalo (buff), which is a species somewhat similar to carp in appearance, and feeding habits as well. While I did manage to land some carp in Texas, they were never too big. Buffs remained elusive for a long time.

Ari and I with a Dallas carp.

For my son's graduation trip, I decided to try fishing for Alligator gar, an exotic species by our standards, that have the potential of reaching 300 lbs. I would have been quite happy with a 100 lbs fish, but that didn't happen. However, Ari and I did land a bunch in the 20 to 60 lbs range, as well as some hybrid gar, which are a cross between longnose and alligator gar.

Alligator gar from the Trinity River, TX.

Over the next few years, I returned to Texas, specifically to fish for big blue catfish in winter. During my first trip there with Ari, we hit an ice storm, which put a serious dent in our plans, but we eventually switched lakes, and managed some decent blue cats up to 33 lbs. The following year, I returned with my two younger sons, Avi and Levi. Weather was a bit better the first day, and they both managed some blue cats in the upper 30 lbs range, but the second day was crazy windy, and we were forced off the water halfway through the outing for safety concerns.

Ari, Avi, and Levi with some big Texas blue cats.

Funny enough, my biggest blue catfish actually came from the James River in Virginia. I had a business trip scheduled near Richmond, and before going I was contemplating driving to the coast for some saltwater fishing. Luckily, one of my carp customers from Virginia put me in touch with a local guide, and being that his rates were low, the venue was close, and fishing was done at night, I didn't run the risk of my meetings running too late to prevent me from fishing. This was back before my Texas catfishing adventures, and while I had caught some small blue cats from shore fishing Texas in the past, these were on another level. I caught my PB that night, a fat 59 lbs blue cat that still remains as my biggest to date.

Between 2013 and 2016, I visited Southwest Colorado with my family a couple times. My in laws had a couple chalets there at the time, which they mainly used during their ski trips in the Rocky Mountains. As I don't ski, I waited for the summer to visit, and for the most part, spent a good chunk of time fishing with my older boys, or solo on occasion. At that altitude, only few trout species can survive, as well as some longnose suckers. At lower elevations, other game fish start to appear, but for the most part, I stuck to small "put and take" style lakes within a 1 hour drive of where we stayed. Most catches were either rainbow or brown trout, though we did manage a bag limit of tasty kokanee salmon during a guided outing to Blue Mesa reservoir at lower altitude.

Our bag limit of tasty kokanee salmon, with some bonus rainbow trout.

Summertime snowmelt above the tree line in the Rockies.

Fast forward a few years to 2020. By then, I had two freshwater species left on my bucket list. The first, was the elusive smallmouth buffalo (buff) I hoped to catch years prior. The other was the monstrous white sturgeon, but that would require a trip to the West coast, and likely hiring a guide's service.

I decided to go for a DIY (do it yourself) style trip to Dallas for buffs. I had credit card points to cover free airfare, and my in laws house to stay at. The only real expense was the car rental and a fishing rod. Prior to travelling, I did some scouting on the Texas fishing forum, of which I had been an active member for a number of years. I was lucky to find Bob, a kind, retired local, who had just taken up fishing for carp and buffs, and had some decent success doing so.

Bob had a very unique setup. An old sailboat he no longer used, docked at a marina in about 25 feet of water on Lake Ray Hubbard, about 25 minutes drive from where I was in Dallas. His "slip" had power, so we would be able to run a heater, lights, or anything else we needed. Best of all, he was able to prebait the spot for himself, as the marina was private access only, and no one else there was fishing at all, let alone for buffs or carp.

Bob and I hit it off nicely, and I was privileged enough to spend 7 out of 8 days fishing with him, pretty much from sunrise to sunset. I finally landed some buffs after some trial and error, and had an amazing time focusing on only fishing for about an entire week, nonstop.

My first "buff", Lake Ray Hubbard TX, February 2020.

The Covid pandemic hit a few weeks after I returned from Dallas, and that put a hold on any travel plans anyone had for a while. By the spring of 2021, travel rules within Canada started relaxing a bit. I figured it would be a perfect time to travel to British Columbia to chase the last freshwater fish on my bucket list, the white sturgeon.

These monstrous, prehistoric creatures can reach 12 feet in length, and weigh over 1000 lbs, though most are a lot smaller than that. I figured catching an 8 footer would be a good target to set, and invited my friend Mike along for the adventure, as he and I had already done a couple big game trips to Florida for saltwater species.

The guides in BC were only too happy to have visitors, as the core of their annual business comes from overseas visitors, which were now barred from visiting due to global travel restrictions due to the pandemic. A couple weeks before the trip, Canada was hit by the second or third Covid wave, and BC imposed travel restrictions between its regions, as well as barring any non work related visits. Luckily, I had a client to visit in BC, who happily obliged, although no one ever checked anything. We simply boarded the flight, got off at Vancouver airport, and headed inland to Chilliwack, which was a short 15 minute drive from where we were launching to fish for white sturgeon for 3 days in a row.

We had some pretty good success fishing for sturgeon, the power in these fish in the strong current of the Fraser River made for some insane battles. On the last day, Mike and I both landed our biggest fish of the trip, with mine slightly bigger at 7 feet 7 inches fork measurement, which was well over 8 feet if you add the tail length. Good enough for me, it was the perfect end to a perfect trip, and my biggest freshwater fish caught to date.

The power of these big sturgeons is insane, due to huge tails and massive head shakes.

Trophy fishing on big waters doesn't always have to be that far from home. On a summer road trip to Toronto in 2022, I booked a day of salmon fishing on Lake Ontario with my son Levi. We launched bright and early, and by sunrise, he and I had landed some nice Chinooks. After a few hours, we headed further offshore, and got into some spectacular Coho salmon and Steelhead fishing, filling a couple coolers full with a good 120-140 lbs of boneless fillets. Needless to say, I tried just about every possible recipe, from marinated, to gravlax, baked, seared, etc. I gave more than a few fillets away to friends and family as well.

Levi and I with some Lake Ontario Chinooks.

Though I've been primarily a freshwater fisherman for most of my life, in my early 40's I decided to finally give big game saltwater fishing a try. With only big predators on my mind, I set three species as my primary bucket list. The goliath grouper, the tarpon, and any species of "big" sharks, made up my "Big 3".

My first big game fishing trip to Florida came in the spring of 2016. After watching some online videos of Ben Chancey from the "Chew on this" channel, I booked his guiding services, and headed down to the Fort Myers / Cape coral area on Florida's West coast. I invited my friend Mike along for our first big game trip together, and luckily for me, he accepted.

As opposed to the deep waters of the Gulf stream off Florida's East coast, the Gulf of Mexico along Florida's coast is shallow, and fishing there can be extremely productive. After catching some stingrays for bait, we headed to fish near some bridge pilings for Goliath groupers. Using an extra heavy Iron man rod, paired to a giant Avet reel spooled with 450 lbs steel cable, horsing these giant, powerful fish with 65 lbs of drag was nothing short of a brutal, two man effort. Still, we achieved our mission, and I had landed my first big game species, a decent 150 lbs or so of Goliath grouper. Unfortunately, we didn't get any shark during that trip, but landed a couple more Goliaths before the trip was over.

My next big game adventure came the following year, in the spring of 2017. Over that winter, I had watched a Florida Adventure Quest TV episode, where the show's host, Jason South, was out with a guide, fishing for big tarpons during the world famous Boca Grande tarpon run. Jason was fighting a nice tarpon in the 150 lbs range, when some big bull sharks surrounded and chomped the tarpon to bits. The guide went shallow, caught a stingray, and headed back to where the bull sharks were at. After baiting the stingray on a heavy shark rod, they managed to land a huge 10 foot bull shark.

At that point, tarpons dropped off my bucket list, as they were just another baitfish when it comes to big sharks. I called the guide from the TV episode (Mike Myers Reelshark Charters), and booked a 2 day trip for my son Avi and I, in hopes of landing at least one big shark. We made our way down to Gasparilla, a small fishing town in Southwest Florida. Unfortunately, the first day ended up way too windy for us to be able to go out to the Boca Grande pass. Using butterfly filleted fresh caught ladyfish as bait, we drift fished for big sharks. We had one bite on the first day, but the shark dropped the line quickly enough. We did manage some other interesting catches while trying to catch bait, a few weakfish (aka sea trout), a decent cobia, and then some. On the second day, we finally made it out to the pass, and ended up landing a huge 9 foot bull shark, estimated to weight over 400 lbs! My 40+ year dream in the making of catching a big shark had finally materialized, and we followed up with a couple smaller blacktip sharks as a bonus.

A couple trips to Florida's West coast landed my First Goliath grouper and some sharks.

Our shark guide mentioned that pound for pound, hammerhead sharks were the best fight, and that South Florida has some absolute giants in the 1000 lbs range. Sure enough, in the spring of 2019, I invited my friends Mike and Yohann, to join me on a quest for some big hammerhead sharks. My older daughter Chani had got married a few months earlier, and had moved to North Miami Beach. I booked our fishing charter out of Fort Lauderdale, so I could spend some time visiting my daughter and son in law as well. Over the course of 3 days of fishing, we trolled for bonitos to use as cutbait, while catching some tasty wahoo, kingfish, and blackfin tuna every now and then. We did manage to land 3 out of 5 sharks, the biggest going about 9 feet long, maybe 250 to 300 lbs. We lost one in the 11-12 foot range as well, but now I had two of the big shark species crossed off my bucket list.

My first Hammerhead shark, April 2019.

Some tasty bi-catches while trolling for shark bait.

I then switched fishing styles for my saltwater trips, doing 3 trips to Key Biscayne, just South of Miami, over the 2 winters in 2021-2022. As opposed to the deep, blue waters of the Gulf stream, most of Key Biscayne is 2-3 feet deep at most, and for the most part, guides use small skiffs with push poles to sight fish.

During my first trip, I brought along my son in law Nati, and his brother Benny. After catching bait, we landed some small bonnet head sharks, followed by a couple blacktip sharks that go ballistic in shallow water. I ended the outing catching a nice barracuda on a topwater lure, after I had been casting for them during much of the day.

Nati with a Bonnethead shark, and my topwater Cuda to end the day.

Next trip to Key Biscayne was a solo outing. The goal was to try sight casting for tarpon, bonefish, and permit. No luck casting in the wind for tarpons, but I did catch the bonefish and a bonnet head shark. The permit were elusive, but I

did manage a very nice Jack Crevalle, and ended the day with another couple blacktip sharks.

For my third trip there the following winter, I brought along my younger daughter Chaya. Besides for visiting my older daughter and grandchildren, we were headed to Orlando to visit Universal studios together. I booked one day on Biscayne bay, hoping to put Chaya onto her first few sharks. We started the day with back to back tarpons on the first few casts, the first was over 100 lbs, and the second a lot bigger, more in the 180 lbs range. While I got a picture with my first tarpon, the second one could not be calmed down enough to grab. I had the leader 3 or 4 times, as the fish fought boat side for about 45 minutes, before fraying the line and popping off. We moved spots, caught some bait, and ended up landing 5 blacktip sharks, and a nice barracuda as well.

The shallow flats of Biscayne Bay produced some toothy critters.

My first tarpon made some crazy jumps in shallow water.

Needless to say, with my daughter living in Miami, I not only have good reason to keep returning there, but a place to stay with amazing fishing all around, both saltwater and freshwater as well. Near her house, there is a small freshwater canal, enlarged to form small "lakes" at some spots. I've managed to land some peacock bass, largemouth bass, and even a Mayan Cichlid there.

Though I love big game fishing in saltwater, sometimes, I'll just opt for a DIY style trip instead, usually when the charters are very expensive, and the chances of success are relatively low. I have very limited saltwater experience as far as fishing from piers, beaches rocks and jetties. As always, that won't stop me from trying.

One of my notable trips was to the island of Kauai in Hawaii back in the summer of 2018. I was there for my sister in laws' wedding, and with the charter operators charging and absolute fortune to maybe have a shot at a big marlin or yellowfin tuna, I opted to bring along some terminal tackle, purchase a rod once there, and fish the various towns on the island, whenever I got the chance. For the most part, I caught a lot of colorful reef fish that were quite small. I baited some of them to night fish for reef sharks, but all I managed to catch on them was a conger eel. Biggest thing I hooked into by accident, was a giant sea turtle that I couldn't even budge in the huge waves. I ended up tightening the drag until it broke my line.

Another fun DIY trip came in the summer of 2023, when my in laws booked us on a family cruise to Bermuda. Once docked, I spent most of my time fishing near the harbor, without even setting foot into town on the main island. Over the course of 2 ½ days, I ended up landing 53 fish of 13 different species. Nothing too big, but some crazy fun in super clear waters.

Some exotic saltwater species caught from shore in Bermuda.

Colorful Hawkfish in Kauai.

DIY trips don't always work out as planned though, so it pays to have a backup plan. During a recent trip, I went to Costa Rica for the first time, where were set to stay at two different jungle locations. The first, was adjacent to a big reservoir named Lake Arenal. I only had one day to fish it, and did so mainly by foot, as well as a couple hours from a small kayak I rented.

The reservoir has to be one of the toughest places I've ever fished. I barely even saw a minnow all day, let alone the "Guapote" (nicknamed rainbow bass) I was after. Most of the locals use handlines and bait to catch anything that bites, and releasing fish is unheard of there. The few locals I managed to speak to, all said that one had to be very lucky to catch anything there.

A couple days later, we headed down the Nicoya peninsula to Santa Teresa beach for a few days. Surf fishing in 6-8 foot waves with a small telescopic bass rod made it very tough to present any lures, and using some snails I found for bait yielded a few small bait sized fish. I spent a good few hours per day shore fishing over 3 days, without much else to show for.

The fishing during that trip was saved by a guided outing I had booked, hoping that some family members would join. Between the early 6:30 am start time, and being on a small boat in the pounding waves, nobody ended up coming along. Though originally planned as an inshore outing, the captain decided to go 20 miles offshore, and we found good success during the last hour or so, with me landing a nice mess of Mahi Mahi, and a mix of yellowfin and skipjack Tuna.

With a good 30 or so fish in the livewell, we headed back to shore, where I helped the captain fillet our catch.

Not only had that miraculous hour or so of fishing saved the entire trip, but I also had enough fish to eat for the remaining 4 days of my stay. I ended up with a large sized Ziplock bag of boneless tuna fillets, and an even larger bag of Mahi Mahi fillets.

Thankfully, fresh tuna is excellent table fare without cooking. A bit of olive oil, fresh squeezed lime, and some salt and pepper, made for some tasty sashimi style eating.

The mahi mahi were slightly more complicated, as they need to be cooked. Luckily, the owner of the resort we stayed at (Nantipa), is not only Jewish, but Shomer Shabbat, and keeps kosher as well. As such, his staff are aware of kashrut and shabbat. They allowed me to "kasher" one of the gas burners in their beachfront restaurant, and bring in my own pan, utensils, and ingredients to their kitchen.

That evening, the seven of us that keep kosher, enjoyed a delicious meal of Mahi Mahi fillets, cooked to perfection. Everyone went for double and even triple servings, and they took the rest of the uncooked Mahi fillets back to their villa where they had a full kitchen to cook them in.

CHAPTER 8

Meaningful catches

I often get asked what the "best" fish I've ever caught was. Best can have many meanings. Longest, heaviest, best tasting, hardest battle, thelist is endless. Looking at my collection of fishing pictures hanging on my office wall, I've often asked myself the same question. Over time, I think that "meaningful" has to be at the top of the list, with "memorable" a close runner up.

Having spent much of my life as a fishing addict, I've caught thousands of fish spanning a vast number of freshwater and saltwater species, in all sorts of circumstances and settings. Where does one even begin determining the top of the list?

I think the answer is a cross between having a dream, setting the goal, and the effort put in to achieve it. Here are some candidates:

My first bass. Fishing as a small child, my late father tied on a small red and white Jitterbug for me to cast, as my hook and sinker setups were getting caught up in rocks too often. Casting along a dropoff from shore, I saw the little smallmouth bass come up in clear water and bust onto my lure. It was at that point where I fell in love with topwater lures and surface bites. I didn't get a picture with that fish, but the topwater passion carried through to some of my more memorable fish later in life.

My obsession with topwater bass fishing started early in life.

Spring of 2009. I still owned my small boat, docked in South Lancaster. My late father was a regular invite on my boat, and for this particular outing, my then 6 year old son Levi came along for the outing, for a day of 3 generation fishing. With winds over 15 km/h, I opted to go up the Raisin River, to fish calmer waters than the wavy St Lawrence, to make for a more enjoyable outing.

We caught a variety of species, and Levi did quite well simply using worms, fished under popping cork rig. At one point, he landed a decent sized crappie, which he posed with for a picture with my dad.

Later on that season, the outdoor Canada magazine launched its first ever picture contest. Having a variety of nice fishing pics, I submitted some for each of us. Sure enough, later that winter, I got a call from the magazine's editor, informing me that Levi's picture had won the grand prize, which was a $1000 USD gift card at Basspro shops.

I did get a variety of gear, some of which we still use, as well as a parka that last me nearly 15 years before I retired it for the 2024 winter season due to wear and tear.

I guess they just couldn't resist the combination of Levi's smile, matched with my dad's old school fisherman look.

"Lucky" Levi and my late father in the winning pic.

In the summer of 2012, my older son Ari and I fished Lac Wahoo at Le Domaine Shannon for the first time. We had a great day, landing countless smaller pike, with a few decent ones mixed in. Towards evening on the first day, I had a giant surface explosion on my Zara spook (topwater lure). The big pike had missed, but came back a second time, and took the lure. It ran straight under the boat ripping drag until the lure popped free. I never did get a glimpse at that pike, but it was definitely well into the double digits. Over many subsequent trips to Lac Wahoo with many of my kids, we did manage to land some big pike, but most came on dead bait before the province wide ban came into effect in 2017. My son Levi did manage a very nice 41 inch / 15 lbs pike on a topwater lure, basically the fish of my dreams, back in the summer of 2018. In the summer of 2020, I did manage another big pike on the zara spook, this time I had it boat side, but my son Eli fumbled the net job, and it got away. Finally, in the summer of 2022, I landed a long 40 inch pike on another topwater lure, the walking mullet. I had waited twelve years for that redemption, and likely fished the lake for about 40 days over that period, before landing a double digit pike on a topwater lure.

Early morning surface bite "walking the dog".

In the summer of 2018, I got my first float tube. It became my latest obsession at the time, and eventually, I coupled it with just about exclusive topwater fishing, which lends itself very well to float tubing for various reasons. Calm days, the lack of electronics, fishing near shorelines, etc. They seem to be tailor made for each other. After a few outings catching mainly bass, I managed to land a small musky on a buzzbait. The catch was totally accidental, I was targeting bass and pike, but it got me thinking about targeting muskies from the float tube using big topwater lures.

The following spring, I scouted a small, calm waterway where I knew I had a slim chance of catching decent sized muskies. Later that summer, I purchased a topraider from my friend Mike, and he gave me a bit of a primer lesson on how to properly use it, also mentioning to try and time my outing with the right solunar time of day (major or minor).

On my first outing to the given spot I had scouted, I timed the major to coincide with the time I estimated to reach my prime spot, a shallower weedy structure that dropped into deeper water. Sure enough, within a couple minutes of reaching the structure, the telltale giant explosion on the big lure signaled success. That musky put up a crazy fight, towing me around in circles. Being on a float tube with the lower half of my body submerged in the water, with a thrashing musky with double treble hooks in its mouth, was quite the experience.

With no room for a landing net on the float tube, I had to wear out the musky a bit more than I wanted to, in order to land it safely. At all costs, I had to avoid getting pinned to the musky and lure, a good hour or so away from any possible help. I was eventually able to grab it by the jaw to land it. To me, that 42.5 ich musky was worth more than the any bigger ones I've caught fishing on my friend's boats.

Unfortunately, it didn't survive the release, so I harvested the fish and had its head mounted. I was not able to ever replicate that success, but to be fair, after a few failed outings, I told myself that it was too risky for the small musky population at my spot for me to target them without proper release gear, especially in warmer water.

On a related note, Rosh Hashana night has always been interesting at my table. This is when we display a fish head, often consumed by those that have the custom to do so. In my house, the debate was always whether or not to cook it. I didn't see the point in cooking it if no one was going to eat it, and all that did was cause it to have a much stronger stench. On the flip side, my wife and older daughter were completely mortified of having a raw severed fish head on the table, despite them hating the smell of a cooked fish head even more than I do.

Catching and harvesting the amount of fish that I do every season, I always made it a goal to save some of the coolest / biggest fish heads for the table, and doing different montages with them for Rosh Hashana. My sons all got a kick out of it, while my wife and daughter complained year after year.

As I was forced to harvest the musky I caught from my float tube, due to it not surviving the battle, I had "Dom's" head mounted, having in mind that I'd have the coolest, odorless Rosh Hashana fish head in town, year after year. No more complaints either.

"Dom" in Rosh Hashana mode.

Another splendid catch, was my biggest carp, a giant 41+ lbs fish I caught back in the spring of 2021. Having caught well over 1000 carp since I first started targeting them in 2006, the 40 lbs club had been elusive up until that point. For this particular outing, I had been pre-baiting my trophy spot for a couple days, and went to fish it with my youngest son Zev, who I was homeschooling at the time. We'd set up the rods, do some studying, and he insisted on netting all the fish. Sure enough, he netted the beast of a carp, which finally hit the size I'd been waiting for, for a good 15 years or so.

My current PB carp.

Then of course, there were the do it yourself success stories like the buffs I landed in Texas, as well as my biggest freshwater and saltwater catches, which came with the help of top notch guides, after lot's of travel and big bucks spent.

Sometimes, it's not necessarily about the biggest catch or best outing. Rather, an unintended by product of a day on the water, which led to other, more meaningful results, unrelated to fishing, or simply a great story. In the summer of 2021, I invited my son Avi to come out float tube fishing with me, something which he has yet to try. He wasn't too interested, so I invited my next son Levi to come along instead. Being a bit more adventurous and free spirited than his older brother, he agreed. We decided on a small lake in the Laurentians, with some crazy numbers of bass, though not many sizeable ones. The outing went as planned, we enjoyed a great afternoon and evening of fishing. As usual, I snapped some pics of us for my blog. A month or so later, my son decided to use the picture on a dating app he was using. Sure enough, the girl he met was attracted to him specifically because of that fishing pic, as she loves eating fish, more than any other food group. They ended up meeting, falling in love, and are now married to each other a couple years later! Not only did that fish end up leading to the catch of a lifetime for him, but lucky for me, I had a pre-scripted fishing story to tell during my speech at their wedding.

Levi's float tube outing netted him a bigger catch in the long run.

Last but not least, my biggest catch on ice. It was just around the start of the Covid pandemic in March of 2020. Quebec started limiting travel to other regions of the province, so I had to adjust my plans accordingly for my last outing of the season. With warming weather and unsafe ice at many local spots, I opted for a spot where I knew I may have a shot at some pike, provided the ice was safe enough. Luckily, I found safe ice, and set up a nice spread of 9 flag lines, baited with frozen mackerels. I saved my 10th line to use for jigging, but the action was super slow. I think all I landed all outing while jigging was one small perch. Around 1 pm, one of my flag lines was tripped. I made my way over to the line, and when I set the hook, I had a good feeling that I was onto what was likely my biggest fish of the winter. Eventually, I got its head near the hole, and realized it was a good sized musky. Though I was fishing 8 inch holes, I was lucky that a nearby feeder creek had thinned the ice to about 6 inches at that particular spot, so I was able to roll up my sleeve, submerge my arm under the ice, and position the big musky's hear facing upwards for me to land it. The musky measured 46 inches, by far my biggest catch on ice up to this point. That ended my ice season on a very high note, just as the entire planet was thrown into the uncertainty and chaos of the early stages of the Covid pandemic. Just about as memorable as one could get.

Epilogue:

As I get up there in age, I find myself being more thankful for every day on the water, especially when my now grown up boys decide to join me. No longer do I have little ones fighting over rods, fish, or space in my car or cabin. These days, I find that I need to convince them to get away from their electronics, cel phones, friends or girlfriends, just to spend time on the water with them. Oh well, I guess it's their loss, maybe one day in the distant future, they'll come to the realization that good times with their dad, don't last forever.

I also find myself being more practical about fishing, and focusing less on the actual quality of many of my outings, as opposed to the "how" of getting there. For example, I can decide to spend a few days prebaiting a spot for carp by bike, instead of driving there by car. Not only do I get a great workout, but the sense of achievement is intensified when it all works out.

Other times, I may opt to fish a tougher lake just for the relaxing drive, nice views, pristine waters, and fresh air. Obviously, the chance at hooking a big fish is always part of the mix, but no longer as much of a sole focus as it once was.

At least I have hope that at some point in the future, I'll have enough grandchildren to initiate into fishing, provided things go as planned. That look of excitement on little faces that I once took for granted, may yet be achievable again someday.

Hopefully sooner, rather than later. Until then, tight lines!

My granddaughter Shaina in training.

www.ingramcontent.com/pod-product-compliance
Lightning Source LLC
Chambersburg PA
CBHW060500010526
44118CB00018B/2481